CONTENTMENT
INSPIRING INSIGHTS FOR LDS MOTHERS

CONTENTMENT
INSPIRING INSIGHTS FOR LDS MOTHERS

MARIA COVEY COLE

Covenant Communications, Inc.

Covenant
Communications, Inc.

To my mother, Sandra Merrill Covey,
who beautifully exemplifies
contentment in motherhood

Cover image: Portrait of Mother and Daughter © Jupiterimages, courtesy of Good Shoot.

Cover design copyrighted 2009 by Covenant Communications, Inc.

Published by Covenant Communications, Inc.
American Fork, Utah

Printed in Canada
First Printing: March 2009

16 15 14 13 12 11 10 09   10 9 8 7 6 5 4 3 2 1

ISBN 13: 978-1-59811-777-6
ISBN 10: 1-59811-777-7

CONTENTS

"O that I were an angel, and could have the wish of mine heart, that I might go forth and speak with the trump of God, with a voice to shake the earth, and cry repentance unto every people! . . . But behold, I am a man, and do sin in my wish; for *I ought to be content* with the things which the Lord hath allotted unto me."
(Alma 29:1, 3; emphasis added)

ACKNOWLEDGMENTS

I would like to express my deepest appreciation to all those who have made the writing and publication of this book possible.

I thank my husband, Dave Cole, who was so helpful and encouraging throughout this entire process. His advice was always on the mark, insightful, and exactly what I needed to hear. Without his help in caring for our children, I wouldn't have had the time or the energy to complete this project. I am so grateful to have a husband who inspires me to fulfill my divine mission.

To my parents, Stephen and Sandra Covey, all of the gratitude in the world is not enough. To paraphrase Abraham Lincoln, "All that I am, and all that I ever hope to be, I owe to my angel [parents]." Their inspired teachings throughout my life have influenced me tremendously in developing the ideology behind this book.

I am deeply indebted to my sisters, Cynthia Haller, Catherine Sagers, Colleen Brown, and Jenny Pitt. They have each spent countless hours reading and rereading my manuscript, editing, giving suggestions, and offering insights of their own. I am truly grateful for their second-mile efforts, born out of love and sisterhood.

My gratitude further extends to my brothers and their spouses: Stephen and Jeri Covey, Sean and Rebecca Covey, David and Pam Covey, and Joshua and Jenny Covey. They have believed in this book from the start, and their enthusiasm and encouragement has meant the world to me.

I offer special thanks to all of the individuals in this book who have allowed me to share their stories. They are inspired and inspiring, and their experiences have greatly enhanced my perspective of what it means to be content.

I am also grateful to my editor, Noelle Perner, who has been extremely patient and kind, and a true advocate on my behalf; my gratitude extends to the entire Covenant team for their valuable contributions.

With deep gratitude, I acknowledge the hand of the Lord in my life. I have been abundantly blessed during the writing of this manuscript, and I am truly grateful for His tender mercies.

INTRODUCTION

> "I wish to say without equivocation that a woman will find no
> greater satisfaction and joy and peace and make no greater
> contribution to mankind than in being a wise and worthy
> woman and raising good children."
>
> —*The Teachings of Spencer W. Kimball*, 327

When I told my friend Anne Workman that I was writing a
book on finding contentment in motherhood, she exclaimed,
"I'm so glad someone is addressing the topic!" She paused a
moment and then continued. "Most of the women I know fall
into one of two camps: the first thinks you must be joking to
suggest that you have to look for contentment as a mother; the
second group is just enduring their time with children at home,
seeing it as a temporary phase in their lives—a break from the
real task of making a living and finding personal fulfillment."

"I fall into the middle," Anne concluded. "I recognize that
the work of mothering is hard, but I believe with all my heart
that it's the best way to bring yourself and your family lasting
joy."

Another friend confided, "I've gone through all of those
feelings of discontent and discouragement. I've questioned
whether I should be doing 'more' with my life. But then I fasted
and prayed that I might truly come to be content with what the
Lord has blessed me with. I've come to feel content with who
and what I am as a mother."

I felt the importance of writing this book more keenly than
ever when I discussed the idea with my niece and she related the
following story: "About a month ago, I went to my book club
where the ladies [all young LDS mothers] were talking about

this very issue. They said that there were some women who could never be happy being mothers and that their work with the world was just as important, if not more so, than that of the mothers of the world. I sat there not saying anything, but their comments bothered me for a long time. The thing that bothered me the most was that I didn't have an intelligent response: I couldn't formulate into words what I was thinking."

After I spoke on this topic in sacrament meeting on Mother's Day, one young mom with three little children approached me cautiously and said, "I didn't know we could talk about this in the Church." When I assured her that contentment was a recurring theme throughout the scriptures, she asked, "Well then, may I have a copy of your talk? I really need to have it by my bedside to review often!"

Over the course of many years and many conversations, I have found that the subject of contentment is near and dear to the hearts of women—especially mothers. Yet this feeling tends to elude us all too frequently. Often, women don't articulate the feelings of discontentment they may have but rather allow them to simmer beneath the surface until they finally boil over in frustration. To make it okay to talk about *finding* contentment validates these very real feelings mothers may have, and it also indicates two things: (1) One has to look for contentment; and (2) Contentment is there for the finding.

George Bernard Shaw wrote: "Life is not about finding yourself. Life is about creating yourself." I stand in awe of my mother, who has raised nine children but has never allowed herself the luxury of "finding herself." When I ask her if she ever felt unfulfilled, discontented, or unappreciated as she was raising us children, she replies, "We didn't ask ourselves those questions in my day. We were happy to be mothers, and we found great fulfillment in our role."

Now, my mother is no shrinking violet. She is incredibly well-read, politically active, smart, engaging, talented, and cultured. (And, as her daughter, I'm not biased at all!) Rather than turning inward to "find" herself, she has "created" herself throughout her life by serving others, building her character, and rising to the challenges life has presented her. At eighteen, my mom was the youngest member of the Mormon Tabernacle Choir; as a collegian, she was selected as the co-valedictorian of the Family Science Department at BYU. At the young age of twenty-five, she was the mission mother to three hundred and fifty missionaries (my dad was a twenty-nine-year-old mission president!) and organized all of the Church auxiliaries throughout Ireland. She has traveled the world and has spoken and sung at countless meetings throughout the Church. She is valiant in her testimony of the restored gospel of Jesus Christ.

Like all mothers, she has had her struggles; rearing nine children is no walk in the park. Still, she understands one thing that many of our generation fail to grasp—contentment in motherhood.

My four sisters and I are all mothers now. Despite our mother's excellent example, we have all struggled to some extent in finding contentment in motherhood. We have all had bouts of feeling overwhelmed, unappreciated, overworked, unnoticed, and underutilized at one time or another. We have a favorite sign displayed in the kitchen of our family cabin that reads, "For this I spent four years in college?"

But as we grow older, and hopefully wiser, those moments of true fulfillment and contentment come much more often and much more powerfully than when we brought home our first little babies and wondered if we were losing ourselves in the process.

I can now truly say that I understand what it means to find contentment in motherhood, and that it is sweet and satisfying beyond anything I could ever have imagined. (My sisters tease that it's because my baby is nine years old!) I've collected quotes and anecdotes about contentment for years, and they have helped me tremendously in coming to the place where I am now.

Perhaps the most important thing I've learned is that contentment is a process. In this little book, I discuss the concepts and principles that have helped me find contentment:

entrusting myself to God's care, gaining perspective, shunning comparison, overcoming discontentment, learning to be content, and, finally, allowing my nature to be changed through the grace of Christ.

Once we learn to feel content as mothers, we can take our lives one step further as we allow our wills to be swallowed up by the will of the Father (see Mosiah 15:7). At that point, our greatest desire becomes to further His cause. Stephen L Richards, a counselor to President David O. McKay, espoused this life motto: "Life is a *mission* and not a career, and the purpose of all our education and knowledge is so that we can better represent Him and serve that mission of life in His name and toward His purposes" (quoted in Stephen R. Covey, *The 8th Habit,* 316; emphasis added). May we find contentment in motherhood as we come to understand and embrace *our* divine mission.

ENTRUSTING OURSELVES TO GOD'S CARE

"Contentment should be the hallmark of the man or woman
who has put his or her affairs in the hands of God."
—Phillip Keller, *A Shepherd Looks at Psalm 23*, 17–18

From this quote by Phillip Keller, we learn that contentment is the "hallmark" of one who has entrusted herself to God's care. But what is contentment? Before we talk more about how to *find* contentment, we need to know what we're looking for.

Defining Contentment

Over the years, I have learned much about the nature of contentment from the scriptures and from the prophets and Apostles. I have come to recognize that contentment comes from being satisfied with "the things which the Lord hath allotted unto me" (see Alma 29:3). I have learned that contentment is an inner peace, a "quiet, inner-soul satisfaction that can steady [you]" (Neal A. Maxwell, *Church News*, Feb. 27, 1983). Contentment is an assurance that your life is acceptable to the Lord and in accordance with His will, and that He approves of your efforts and the course you are pursuing, "notwithstanding [your] weakness" (2 Nephi 33:11).

I have also learned what contentment is *not*. Contentment is not complacency, mediocrity, smugness, or settling for something less. President Gordon B. Hinckley said, "I have been quoted as saying, 'Do the best you can.' But I want to emphasize that it be the very best. We are too prone to be satisfied with mediocre performance. We are capable of doing so much better" ("Standing Strong and Immovable," Worldwide Leadership Training Meeting, Jan. 2004, 21).

When I was a junior in high school, our drama department put on Thornton Wilder's stage production of *Our Town*. I remember the play well because I was cast as Howie Newsome's wife. To give you an idea of how central to the plot my part was, Howie Newsome was the town milkman, and his wife wasn't even on the list of characters! Oh, well. Both then and now, this play has taught me much about the meaning of contentment.

Our Town is set in the fictional town of Grover's Corners, New Hampshire, in 1901; however, Grover's Corners could have been any small town, really, and the townspeople of Grover's Corners could have been found in any American town of that era. Wilder stages the play very simply, with minimal props, and introduces the town and its characters through a stage manager who acts as the narrator. At the center of the play are two families: the Gibbses and the Webbs. They live side by side on the same quiet street, and their lives are thoroughly intertwined.

In the first act of the play, Wilder portrays many of the characters' daily routines. As the curtains open, we see the residents of Grover's Corners waking up, having breakfast, reading the paper, getting ready for and rushing off to work and school, doing mundane chores, and so on. Howie Newsome, the milkman, delivers the morning's order of milk. Joe Crowell Jr., the paperboy, makes his neighborhood rounds. Doc Gibbs returns from an exhausting night of delivering a set of twins in Polish town. Mrs. Gibbs feeds her chickens from her apron while Mrs. Webb strings beans. Just a typical morning filled with unremarkable details. We note a certain simplistic, predictable, yet secure routine in this town and within these families.

The stage manager's narration jumps forward in time to late afternoon, and we witness an interchange between teenagers

Emily Webb and George Gibbs on their way home from school. George suggests that he and Emily devise a communication system between their two homes, from his upstairs window to hers, so that she can help him with his algebra. The audience can sense their apparent yet unexpressed affection for one another. That night, as they sit on their window sills and talk across the way, they point out how beautiful the moon looks.

The second act takes place three years later on George and Emily's wedding day. George tries to sneak a peek at Emily before the ceremony, but he is shooed away by Mr. and Mrs. Webb, who remind him that it is bad luck to see the bride-to-be on her wedding day. George has an awkward conversation with his future father-in-law about marriage and what it takes to be a good husband. Although both George and Emily are nervous and anxious about getting married, their parents offer reassurance and encourage them to go through with the ceremony. The stage manager acts as the minister as they are lovingly joined together in holy matrimony.

The next and final act of the play happens nine years later. The setting is a cemetery on a hill overlooking the tiny town of Grover's Corners. Emily has died giving birth to her second child and is about to be buried. She is only twenty-six years old. As a spirit, Emily meets some of her former friends and townspeople, including her mother-in-law, Mrs. Webb. The grieving funeral party comes forward from the back of the stage. The dead souls all watch this procession in an indifferent manner, seemingly unaffected by the anguish of those in attendance at Emily's funeral.

Only Emily is moved, and she reaches out in compassion to her family and friends. Despite the warnings of the departed souls surrounding her, Emily announces that she wants to go back to earth to revisit her life one last time before resigning herself to the disconnected existence of the dead. The stage manager tells her that she can choose one day in her life to which she may return. She chooses an ordinary yet somewhat special day: her twelfth birthday.

The next scene opens on the humble town Emily has always known. But somehow, Grover's Corners now seems remarkable and extraordinary, and Emily delights in identifying all of its memorable landmarks. She is transported to the kitchen of her family home, where her mother is calling the children to breakfast. Emily is amazed by how young her mother looks. She listens intently to the trivial conversation between her parents, delighting in each word. More in wonder than in grief, Emily cries out, "I love you all—everything. I can't look at everything hard enough" (97). In response to her mother imploring her to eat a good breakfast, birthday or no birthday, Emily replies, "Oh, Mama, just look at me one minute as though you really saw me" (99). Just then, she hears her father's voice calling her.

Abruptly, Emily turns to the stage manager and declares, "I can't. I can't go on. It goes so fast. We don't have time to look at one another" (100). She begs to be taken back up the hill to her grave.

As she leaves earth life for the last time, Emily cries out, "Oh, earth, you're too wonderful for anybody to realize you." Imploringly, she asks the stage manager, "Do any human beings ever realize life while they live it?—every, every minute?" The stage manager answers, "The saints and poets, maybe—they do some" (100).

Emily rejoins the other spirits in the cemetery. The dead sit silently in the darkness, enjoying the companionship of the stars. George Gibbs approaches Emily's grave and throws himself upon it in anguish. Emily looks sorrowfully at Mrs. Gibbs, who has also passed away, and asks, "They don't understand, do they?" Mrs. Gibbs replies, "No dear. They don't understand" (103).

In the closing scene, the stage manager reports that nearly everybody is now asleep in Grover's Corners. He acknowledges that here on earth, everyone strains to make something of life and that "the strain's so bad that every sixteen hours everybody lies down and gets a rest" (103). The stage manager looks at his watch and tells us that it is now eleven o'clock. After a pause, he suggests that the audience return home and that they too get some rest. It is a fitting conclusion to a powerful play.

The final act of *Our Town* underscores the focus of Wilder's play: to encourage us to live life to its fullest; to realize the significance of human interaction; to cherish the simple, small moments of everyday existence that we so often take for granted. When Emily is given the opportunity to revisit her life, she recognizes that the most important moments and the most worthwhile experiences in life are found in the simple routines of a single day.

Since being part of this play as a teenager, I have had many *Our Town* moments, and I try to recognize and appreciate the significance of each one. I have come to understand that the echo of eternity is found in each and every human being and in the interactions between human beings, and that we must not allow these small yet significant moments to pass by without valuing them.

That is why I treasure holding my newborn babies, delight in chasing my toddlers around the house, prize going on Sunday walks with my middle children, and relish spending time with my teenagers. All of these simple, ordinary moments of daily life are precious and are to be savored. And for a mother, this is where true contentment is ultimately found.

Allowing God to Direct Our Path

When I look back on my life and recall the times that I've felt the most content, the most happy and fulfilled, I recognize that these were the times when I entrusted myself to God's care and allowed Him to direct my path. In these moments, I was "dissolved into something complete and great" (Willa Cather, *My Antonia*, 20).

For instance, as a twenty-one-year-old missionary in Ireland, I experienced deep and lasting contentment as I followed the Spirit's promptings to serve a mission and was given the opportunity to teach and testify, to search for, and find those whom the Lord had prepared to hear His word. Though we had little success baptism-wise, I had never felt so fulfilled, so happy, and so full of purpose.

Later, marriage and children brought similar, enduring feelings of contentment and purpose. As a young wife and mother, I felt the need for the Lord's guidance and care more keenly than ever; as I entrusted myself and my family to His care, I better understood my purpose and the importance of my role as a wife and mother. I knew deep within my heart that this was what life was all about, and through the years I've found great fulfillment in these roles.

However, at times during my adulthood, the "five metastasizing cancers," as my father calls them—comparing, competing, criticizing, complaining, and complacency—have reared their ugly heads in an effort to divert me from my divine mission and discourage me from accepting the Lord's guidance. I've found that engaging in *any* of these behaviors can lead to feelings of discontentment. Unless we are particularly vigilant, it is easy to, as the saying goes, get caught up in the "thick of very thin things," ultimately distracting us from the true purpose of life. I've been inspired and profoundly changed by the following quotation by Christian writer Malcolm Muggeridge, who reminds us so eloquently of the things that matter most:

> When I look back on my life nowadays, which I sometimes do, what strikes me most forcibly about it is that what seemed at the time most significant and seductive, seems now most futile and absurd. For instance, success in all its various guises; being known and being praised; ostensible pleasures, like acquiring money or seducing women, or traveling, going to and fro in the world and up and down in it like Satan, exploring and experiencing whatever Vanity Fair has to offer.
>
> In retrospect, all these exercises in self-gratification seem pure fantasy, what Pascal

called "licking the earth." They are diversions designed to distract our attention from the true purpose of our existence in this world, which is, quite simply, to look for God, and, in looking, to find Him, and, having found Him, to love Him, thereby establishing a harmonious relationship with His purposes for His creation. (Quoted in Neal A. Maxwell, "A Christ-Centered Life," *Ensign*, August 1981, 13)

In other words, lasting contentment comes from pursuing the true reasons for our existence: looking for, finding, loving, and serving God and His children. All other pursuits are mere distractions. Heavenly Father will help us discern worthy pursuits and sources of true contentment and joy as we entrust ourselves to His care and allow Him to guide our lives.

Finding Contentment in Spite of Difficulty
One of the distinguishing traits of a Latter-day Saint woman should be a serene sense of gentle contentment. As we read in 1 Timothy 6:6, "Godliness with contentment is great gain." As God's children, we should be completely satisfied with His guidance in our lives: "The Lord is my shepherd; I shall not want" (Psalm 23:1). Yet, too often we are neither satisfied nor content, and the reason we generally offer is that life hasn't turned out the way we'd planned. Life is different from—and sometimes much harder than—what we'd expected.

This is particularly true of motherhood. I remember when I was a single young adult, stressed out by the demands of graduate school, work, and dating relationships, I would often visit my older sister, who lived close to the university. She was married and a mother to two little girls whom she adored but who were wearing her out, and she grumbled a little bit about not having enough time for herself because of the demands of her family. I asked her incredulously, "How could *you* possibly be dissatisfied? You have a wonderful husband and beautiful children—two things that I want and don't have. How can a person ever wish for more when she has everything there is worth having?" She mumbled something about how I was right, of course, and that she really *was* grateful for the blessings she'd been given. In retrospect, I'm impressed that she didn't take offense by my complete disregard for the struggles she was going through.

Fast forward a half dozen years. I now had a husband and two toddlers of my own, and I too was frustrated, finding it utterly exhausting to keep the kids occupied with productive and rewarding activities every day. I remember thinking, *Why didn't anyone ever tell me that as a mother I'd have to entertain my kids all day long?* Their infancy, which I had initially found terrifying and overwhelming, now seemed so much easier: The baby would just sit and smile and coo, and he couldn't escape. "Oh, why didn't I appreciate the 'simplicity' of that stage?" I would moan.

It seems to be the lot of mankind that we fail to recognize the beauty and worth inherent within each phase of life we pass through. It was M. Scott Peck, in *The Road Less Traveled,* who stated, "Life is difficult. . . . Once we truly know that life is difficult—once we truly understand and accept it—then life is no longer difficult. Because once it is accepted, the fact that life is difficult no longer matters" (15).

Elder Henry B. Eyring makes it clear that Heavenly Father's plan was explained to us in the spirit world before we were born, and that although we knew the test would be difficult, we "rejoiced" at the opportunity to show our faith and obedience because we had confidence that we could prevail. He reminds us, "On many days, doing what matters most will not be easy. It is not supposed to be. God's purpose in creation was to let us prove ourselves. . . . 'And we will prove them herewith, to see if they will do all things whatsoever the Lord their God shall command them' (Abraham 3:25)" ("This Day," *Ensign,* May 2007, 89–90).

Similarly, understanding and accepting that motherhood is intrinsically challenging and demanding somehow makes it more manageable. Everything the Lord asks of His children, though difficult, is for our good, for our advancement, and for our motivation, to spur us on to greater achievement. The potential within us will be properly developed as we entrust ourselves to God's care and choose to be satisfied with His guidance despite the fact that we may find ourselves in difficult or trying situations. Every day, as we petition our Father in Heaven, we should talk to Him and listen to His counsel, for it is the counsel that *He* gives that we must follow—not the determination of our own desires or interests.

As daughters of God, when we acknowledge His goodness and mercy in our lives, accept that life is not meant to be easy, and learn that motherhood is, by divine design, difficult and testing, we will truly be content with the things the Lord has allotted to us.

GAINING PERSPECTIVE

"If we work upon marble, it will perish. If we work upon brass, time will efface it. If we rear temples, they will crumble into dust. But if we work upon immortal minds, and instill into them just principles, we are then engraving on that tablet that which no time will efface, but will brighten and brighten to all eternity."
—Daniel Webster, as quoted in Stephen R. Covey, *The 7 Habits of Highly Effective Families,* 75

An important aspect of finding contentment in our lives is gaining perspective. As we learn to view motherhood through the eternal lens of the gospel, we can create a legacy of joy within our homes, and we will exemplify to our families our belief in the transcendent significance of motherhood.

Creating a Legacy of Joy

One of my favorite books (which has been made into an exceptional movie) is entitled *Eleni.* It's the true story of a woman who is driven to extraordinary actions out of love for her children. The story takes place in 1948 as civil war ravages Greece and a communist attachment terrorizes a small mountain village by abducting the children and sending them to communist camps behind the Iron Curtain. Eleni Gatzoyiannis defies the communist uprising and arranges for the escape of her three daughters and her son, Nicola. For this act she is imprisoned, tortured, and executed in cold blood.

Thirty years later, Nicola, who has become a reporter for *The New York Times,* returns to his homeland to learn the facts surrounding his mother's death and to hunt down the man who tried and executed her. As he does his investigative work, he

learns about the last days of his mother's life through people
from his village who knew Eleni and witnessed her execution.
Scenes from the past are opened up to Nicola, and he learns
about the character and commitment of his devoted mother.

A particularly touching scene depicted in the movie
portrays the night before Eleni is to be executed. The guard
allows Eleni's second oldest daughter, who has been forcibly
enlisted into the communist regime, to visit and spend one last
moment with her mother. The daughter, only fifteen years old,
collapses into her mother's arms and expresses a desire to die.
Eleni holds her up, looks deeply into her eyes, and pleads, "You
must live! You have something wonderful to look forward to.
Someday, you will marry and have children of your own. *It is
such a joy to be a mother.*" This hope and unconditional love
strengthens the daughter, and she promises Eleni that she *will*
live and become a mother someday.

On the day Eleni is executed, she courageously stands in
front of the firing squad and voices one last cry that echoes
throughout the hills as the bullets pierce her body: "My children!"

When Nicola learns of the details of his mother's death and
of the courage of her life, he becomes incapable of revenge
because of the depth of her love for him and his siblings. He
realizes that his mother's love is a legacy she has bequeathed to
him, and that the choice to leave that same legacy to his own
children is now his.

I sometimes wonder if my children know from my example
and expressions that it is "such a joy to be a mother." Or, rather,
do they view motherhood as difficult and mundane? What attitudes about motherhood am I creating in my home? If my children observe my selfless actions and attitude, it is likely that
they too will become selfless. Conversely, if they observe selfish-
ness, then they too may become selfish. What will be the legacy
that I bequeath to my children?

In a recent conversation I had with Lynn, a mother of
eleven grown children, she expressed regret that while raising

her children she had not articulated her feelings about mother-hood often enough. She told me that she had loved being a mother and had always felt happy and fulfilled in her role, yet she was so busy keeping up with life and getting through the years that she had never really taken the time to make a point of it. She now feels distressed that her daughters, who have recently become mothers themselves, seem unhappy and discontent. She wishes that when her girls were younger she had been more verbal in expressing to them the significance of motherhood and the joy she experienced in being a mother.

Understanding the Transcendent Significance of Motherhood

As mothers, we sometimes feel that our influence is infinites-imal. The work we do within the walls of our own homes is rarely recognized, let alone celebrated. We wonder about the contribution we could make if we were out in the world—the causes we could champion, the people we could assist.

Yet, we may find comfort in a statement made by Dag Hammarskjold, an international diplomat who served for eight years as the secretary-general of the United Nations. At the conclusion of a lifetime of service to his fellow men, he shared this profound insight: "It is more noble to give yourself completely to one individual than to labor diligently for the salvation of the masses" (quoted in Stephen R. Covey, *The 7 Habits of Highly Effective People,* 201).

Giving yourself completely to each individual in the family is the very definition of mothering. Latter-day Saint mothers can come to better understand the transcendent significance of motherhood as they recognize that each individual child with whom they have been entrusted is a beloved spirit son or daughter of God with a divine nature and destiny and who is, as such, precious beyond measure. "Remember the worth of souls is great in the sight of God" (D&C 18:10).

I love the perspective my sister Catherine shared with me on this subject. She said, "The unique thing about motherhood is that we can literally influence generations. No other job in the world is like that. Society fails to recognize this, however, and so mothers are encouraged to go out into the world and accomplish something to show for *themselves*. What mothers don't often realize is that their children are their accomplishments! They are like the promotions that others receive and the trophies that others have won." The scriptures foretell additional rewards for selfless mothering: "Her children [will] arise up, and call her blessed; her husband also, and he praiseth her" (Proverbs 31:28).

I remember reading "Bits and Pieces," an autobiographical account of my grandmother's life, and being touched by her example of wholehearted devotion to her family, as well as her perspective on the importance of her calling. "Grandy" states that the greatest contribution she felt she could make to society was to raise good children—and she did. She truly poured herself into each child, so much so that my father has expressed that never has he felt such a constant source of love. "I knew she always loved me, and that love sustained me," he said.

President Gordon B. Hinckley was an exceptionally strong advocate for mothers. The respect and devotion he showed to his wife, Marjorie, over nearly sixty-seven years of marriage is evidence of the high esteem in which he held women. He had this to say about mothers: "We frequently speak of the strength of the priesthood, and properly so. But we must never lose sight of the strength of the women. It is mothers who set the tone of the home. It is mothers who most directly affect the lives of their children. It is mothers who teach infants to pray, who read to them choice and beautiful literature from the scriptures and other sources. It is mothers who nurture them and bring them up in the ways of the Lord. Their influence is paramount" ("Standing Strong and Immovable," Worldwide Leadership Training Meeting, Jan. 2004, 20).

Elder M. Russell Ballard reiterated this sentiment in his assertion that "there is no role in life more essential and more eternal than that of motherhood" ("Daughters of God," *Ensign,* May 2008, 108).

As the principal teacher and nurturer in the home, there is no limit to the influence a righteous mother may have upon the lives of her children. Julie Beck, Relief Society general president, spoke of meeting a group of righteous, young, "covenant-keeping" mothers at a park. She noted that they were bright, university-educated women who had now shifted their considerable talents to raising their children. She watched as they soothed babies, wiped tears, and taught two-year-olds how to share.

When Sister Beck asked one of these young women how she was able to transfer her efforts so cheerfully to motherhood, the young woman replied, "I know who I am, and I know what I am supposed to do. The rest just follows."

Impressed by her perspective of the eternal significance of motherhood, Sister Beck predicted: "That young mother will build faith and character in the next generation one family prayer at a time, one scripture study session, one book read aloud, one song, one family meal after another. She is involved in a great work. She knows that 'children are an heritage of the Lord' and 'happy is the [woman] that hath [a] quiver full of them' (Psalm 127:3, 5). She knows that the influence of righteous, conscientious, persistent, daily mothering is far more lasting, far more powerful, far more influential than any earthly position or institution invented by man" ("A Mother Heart," *Ensign*, April 2004, 77).

Upon publishing her first novel, Jaroldeen Edwards, mother of twelve, was interviewed by two attractive and sophisticated New York women, both graduates of prestigious Ivy League schools, and both successful journalists.

Sister Edwards wrote of the interview:

> I must confess that I was a little chagrined as the morning progressed. I was trying so hard to give the appearance of a professional writer, but every few minutes one of my children would pop into the living room with a problem or a

question. My boys were playing a noisy game in the family room, the stereo was on in the basement play room, and the phone would not stop ringing. Neighborhood friends ran in and out the doors, and finally, my 5-year-old (who had had enough of having to "stay out of the living room") came bouncing in with a smile and plunked herself down on my lap.

We had finished the interview, which had taken about two hours, and the reporters got up to leave. The younger one asked if she could use my phone. As she left, the cool and sophisticated senior reporter walked over and sat down on the couch next to me.

"There's something I want to tell you," she said intensely.

I looked at her in surprise. Very slowly, she said, "I just want you to know that we were sold a lie."

"What do you mean?" I asked, totally puzzled.

"I mean, when I went to college they lied to us," she replied. "They told us we were brilliant, and that we had the obligation to seek success. We were told not to throw our lives away on husbands and children, but to go out into the world and succeed. We were told that only through a professional career could we 'find ourselves' or live a worthwhile life. . . .

"This morning I have realized it was all a lie. I have come to know that a career is not a life— it is only something you do until you find a life. Life is what you are. . . .

"I would trade all my so-called worldly success for one day of living your life." (*Church News*, Mar. 1990, 8, 10)

It is said that "No man on his deathbed wishes he had spent more time at the office." At the end of the day, people recognize that the contentment and happiness they have experienced in life are the rewards of sacrificing for and loving others. When a mother truly comprehends the significance of what she does each day and the influence for good she has upon her children, she takes the first step on the pathway to contentment.

Viewing Motherhood through the Lens of the Gospel

Several years ago, Rebecca Pitt, a close friend of mine, was selected as the English Sterling Scholar for her high school. She had such outstanding credentials and performed so well at region and district competitions that she found herself in the final round at state, competing against two other girls for the coveted, prize-winning scholarship.

In the final interview, three intimidating male judges asked Rebecca this important question: "If we award you this scholarship, what do you plan to do with it?" Rebecca answered truthfully that she planned to pursue an undergraduate degree in English at an excellent university, and that after that she would love to continue her education and ultimately receive a master's degree as well. She expressed her love for learning and her desire to write, edit, and teach, but she conceded that after she married and had children, motherhood would be her first priority.

The judges were noticeably upset by her answer. One refuted, "Why would we waste a scholarship on you if you don't plan to use your education for anything useful?" Rebecca was shocked by his response. Having been raised in a home where motherhood was not only valued but recognized as the most important achievement she could ever attain, she was taken aback by these men's lack of perspective.

Rebecca later reported, "I lost, but I didn't feel too bad about it. Even at the young age of seventeen, I knew the difference an educated mom can make in the world."

I had a similar experience with my daughter Hannah when she was a fifteen-year-old ninth grader. I was summoned to the annual SEOP (Student Educational/Occupational Plan) meeting with the academic counselor at the junior high school. Hannah was already sitting in his office when I arrived and saw that they had been perusing her recent scores from the latest standardized achievement test. The counselor exclaimed, "Hannah, these are outstanding test scores, and you have such excellent grades! You have to at least get a bachelor's and then a master's degree. You could pursue any career you wish with marks like these." Noticing that she remained quiet despite his enthusiastic roadmap for her future, the counselor finally asked, "Well, what are your plans?"

Not realizing how culturally incorrect she sounded, Hannah answered without pretense, "I want to be a mom."

Never have I been more proud of Hannah than I was at that moment. Of course Hannah will go to college and pursue a bachelor's and possibly a master's degree. Of course her father and I want her to gain knowledge and to learn skills that will qualify her to make a living in the field of her choice. Our latter-day prophets have been exceptionally clear about the importance of young women gaining as much education and qualifications for employment as they possibly can, particularly in light of statistics that show that women often need to help support their families financially for one reason or another (see Gordon B. Hinckley, "Seek Learning," *New Era,* Sept. 2007, 4). However, we have also been taught that motherhood is the most important job we can prepare for. And ultimately, the desire and motivation to accept this calling must come from within. And I felt pleased that at that moment, Hannah had a true desire to be a mother.

Isn't it a compelling testament to the divinely appointed role of women that most little girls are, without intervention, innately drawn to womanly roles of mothering and nurturing? We see this evidenced by the way they play with dolls and take care of babies. My brother Stephen teased his five-year-old daughter, Arden, recently, saying, "What are you going to be when you grow up? A basketball player or a soccer player, or do you still want to be a princess?" She answered, "No, Daddy. I want to be a mommy."

Yet something often happens between those early childhood years and the time a young woman is ready to marry and have children. The philosophies of the world are introduced, enticing her away from her eternal calling as wife and mother. Popular TV programs, talk shows, and almost any other form of popular media is filled to the brim with the selfish attitudes and beliefs of society, inundating women with the message that it is not enough to be only a mother—they must pursue a glamorous career to find themselves and to be fulfilled as women rather than adopting the scriptural perspective that to find their life they must lose it in the service of others.

This doesn't mean that it is wrong to have dreams or aspirations in addition to those of being a wife and mother. On the contrary, our Heavenly Father has blessed all of His daughters with intellect, talent, and ability, and He wants to see us magnify these God-given gifts. The key is to remember that "to every thing there is a season, and a time to every purpose under the heaven" (Ecclesiastes 3:1).

I recently heard Dr. Brent Barlow, professor of marriage and family science at BYU, speak about the stages of marriage. He asked the audience, "Do you realize that you only have your children at home for less than *half* of your married life? The other half you are alone with your spouse." He went on to express his belief that if parents—particularly mothers—understood this, they would not be as anxious for their children to grow up so soon. Once children are gone, parents often regret that they did not more fully enjoy their children while they were at home.

Elder M. Russell Ballard addressed this very issue in a recent conference talk directed to young mothers:

> I am impressed by countless mothers who have learned how important it is to focus on the things that can only be done in a particular

season of life. . . . It is crucial to focus on our children for the short time we have them with us and to seek, with the help of the Lord, to teach them all we can before they leave our homes. . . . I believe that the instincts and the intense nurturing involvement of mothers with their children will always be a major key to their well-being. In the words of the proclamation on the family, "Mothers are primarily responsible for the nurture of their children." ("Daughters of God," *Ensign,* May 2008, 108)

All of us have dreams, both large and small, for our lives. Yet some of these aspirations may remain latent for a little while because the Lord's timetable and plan for our lives is often different from our own imaginings. Yet, as we see our lives and calling as mothers through the lens of the gospel, we will gain understanding, and we will be richly blessed for making motherhood our highest priority during certain "seasons" of our lives. While we cannot do it all at the same time, we can do it all *eventually.* If our desires are righteous and we strive to achieve our goals with all of our heart, might, mind, and strength, God will help us fulfill these righteous desires—in due time.

As we come to better understand gospel teachings and see our lives in the light that they afford, we will find ourselves more content in our calling as mothers and in our circumstances in life. President Boyd K. Packer stated this principle beautifully in a general conference address. He said, "True doctrine, understood, changes attitudes and behavior" ("Little Children," *Ensign,* Nov. 1986, 17). I can't think of a better example to illustrate the truth of this statement than "The Family: A Proclamation to the World," which was issued by the First Presidency and the Quorum of the Twelve Apostles in September of 1995. The veracity of this document and its timing were truly inspired as we have seen the very definition of the family come under fire in the ensuing years. This "true doctrine" has greatly influenced the attitudes and behavior of Latter-day Saints in countless ways. And it is imperative that we continue to teach these doctrines to the women *and* young women of the Church in order to point out the clear discrepancy between the teachings of the world and the teachings of the Lord concerning the role of mothers.

Susan Tanner, former Young Women general president, recounted an experience she had years ago with her then sixteen-year-old daughter. She had asked her daughter what she liked best about the recent general conference. Her daughter replied, "I loved it! I loved hearing inspired, intelligent prophets and leaders affirm motherhood." Then she told her parents that this was one of the most "disturbing anxieties" of her life: "I just don't hear it from anyone—not at seminary, not in Young Women, and definitely not at school; nowhere except at home."

Sister Tanner went on to say that alarming though it may be, her daughter's experience is most likely the norm among our young women. "I know that for some time it has not been vogue for women to extol the virtues of motherhood or for young women to express the desires of their hearts to be mothers" ("Strengthening Future Mothers," *Ensign,* Oct. 2004, 20–24).

If this is literally the case, then it is *incumbent* upon the mothers and Young Women leaders of our day to often express how noble it is to be a mother and to unequivocally affirm what President Kimball taught: "A woman will find no greater satisfaction and joy and peace and make no greater contribution to mankind than in being a wise and worthy woman and raising good children" (*Teachings,* 327). We must further exemplify in our own homes what it means to be a "joyful mother of children" (Psalm 113:9). If we, as LDS women, do not value motherhood and hold it in the highest esteem, who will? We must lead in our duty to glorify motherhood.

My sister Jenny, a mother of four young children, decided to make a point of verbalizing her love for motherhood and the significance of her "job" in the world today. Her son, Preston, had "career day" in his first-grade class, and Jenny signed up to talk to the children about her important career. Many other parents had already shared their experiences as lawyers, doctors, dentists, nurses, accountants, retail managers, and members of other professions.

Jenny started by telling the kids that she had the best job in the whole world and that she wanted them to guess what she did. The children threw out all sorts of things they considered to be ideal jobs: pizza delivery person, doctor, vet, baker, dentist, teacher, banker, singer, dancer, professional basketball player, etc. After listing all of these careers on the board, Jenny claimed that she did all of them! The class didn't believe her, so she explained, "I'm a mom, and it is the best job in the world because I get to do *all* of these things. I bandage cuts, I play hoops with my kids, I sing and dance with my girls, I help with homework, I make dinners, I take care of pets, I save and balance the money, and I pull teeth."

She talked about all of the things mothers do—starting with the ordinary and mundane tasks: cleaning, cooking, changing diapers, doing laundry, carpooling, and more. She then focused on the best parts of her job: reading with her kids, playing hide-and-seek, drawing pictures and mailing them to loved ones, taking care of a sick baby in the night, singing songs as her children fall asleep, decorating her house for holidays, and being there for the little but important moments that she wouldn't want to miss. By the time she was finished, she had the students convinced that being a mother was the best profession around. In fact, Jenny even heard her son, Preston, bragging to his friends, "My mom's got the best job!"

In her insightful general conference talk, "A Mother Heart," Sister Julie Beck summed up the dilemma between the pull of the world versus the pull of the home by describing the gospel-centered perspective LDS mothers are blessed with:

> Rather than listening to the voices and partial
> truths of the world, [a woman with a mother
> heart] knows that gospel standards are based on

eternal, unchangeable truths. She believes that to be "primarily responsible for the nurture of [her] children" is a vital, dignified, and "sacred responsibility" ("The Family: A Proclamation to the World"). To nurture and feed them physically is as much an honor as to nurture and feed them spiritually. She is "not weary in well-doing" and delights to serve her family, because she knows that "out of small things proceedeth that which is great." (*Ensign,* May 2004, 76)

The inspired counsel that we as LDS mothers constantly receive from our leaders about the family, thanks to latter-day revelation, helps us maintain a proper perspective so that we are not adversely affected by every changing wind of doctrine introduced by the world. And as we see motherhood through the lens of the gospel, we will be better able to find contentment in our calling and leave a legacy of joy to the children that we raise.

SHUNNING COMPARISON AND STRENGTHENING OTHERS

"Always be a first-rate version of yourself, instead of a second-rate version of somebody else."

—Judy Garland

Some of the most destructive behaviors women engage in include comparing themselves to and competing with others. For some reason, mothers are particularly susceptible to these unhealthy patterns. All too often, we allow ourselves to feel inadequate, or we adopt the attitude that we "just don't measure up" to the women around us. Rather than looking inward for self-acceptance, however, we must instead look to the Lord for an eternal perspective of our divine worth. Only then are we free to recognize the goodness in others and to strengthen those around us.

Recognizing the Importance of Never Comparing Ourselves or Our Families with Others
President Spencer W. Kimball was the prophet of my youth. I loved and admired him so much during those formative years that I was surprised to run across this story. Norma Ashton, wife of Elder Marvin J. Ashton, recounted:

 Spencer W. Kimball and Harold B. Lee were close friends. They went into the Quorum of the Twelve just a few weeks apart. President Kimball said he always admired this friend so very much; in fact, he almost envied President

Lee for his talents. He took every occasion to
tell President Lee how he felt. Often he would
say, "Harold, I wish I could play the organ as
you do." "Harold, you speak so well. I wish I
could do as well." "Harold, you can see the gist
of a problem in such a short time. I wish my
mind were so clear." Then, related President
Kimball, in one of their weekly meetings in the
temple President Lee made a fine presentation
to the other members of the Twelve. As they
walked out of the temple together, again
President Kimball turned to his friend and said,
"You did a magnificent job with your report this
morning. I wish I could do as well as you do."
"Well," said President Kimball with a twinkle in
his eyes, "I guess Harold had had enough. He
stopped, put his hands on his hips, and looking
me straight in the eye, said, 'Spencer, the Lord
doesn't want you to be a Harold B. Lee. All he
wants is for you to be the best Spencer W.
Kimball you can be.'" With a smile on his face,
President Kimball said, "Ever since then I have
just tried to be the best Spencer W. Kimball I
can be."

At the conclusion of this account, Sister Ashton wisely
summed up, "All the Lord asks of us is to be the best we can be
with what we have. . . . As Spencer W. Kimball was taught, a
copy is never as valuable as the original. Each of us is an original
made by God, and we diminish ourselves and our Maker when
we question our worth" ("For Such a Time as This," *The Best of
Women's Conference,* 17–18).

I remember President Kimball being one of the most chari-
table people I had ever observed. People who knew him say that
he emanated love like no other, that when you were in his presence you felt the love of the Savior. He would often embrace
and even give a sweet kiss to those who met him. Each time, he

would say, "I love you." His sermons were powerful and bold, while his delivery was always sensitive and tender. He was a man of action. "Do it!" was the motto he prominently displayed on his desk. To think that such a person often felt inadequate and compared himself to another was amazing to me!

Elder Paul H. Dunn suggested that it is human nature for us to be painfully aware of our own inadequacies and to compare ourselves with others. He wrote:

> I have noticed that daily we meet moments that steal our self-esteem. They are inevitable. Pick up any magazine; you see people who look healthier, skinnier, or better dressed than you are. Look around. There is always someone who seems smarter, another more self-assured, and still another more talented. In fact, each day we are reminded that we lack certain talents, that we make mistakes, that we do not excel in all things. And amidst all this, it is easy to believe that we do not quite measure up in the great scheme of things, but are inferior in some secret way. . . .
>
> If you base your self-esteem, your feeling of self-worth, on anything outside the quality of your heart, your mind, or your soul, you have based it on a very shaky footing. So you and I are not perfect in form or physical figure? So you and I are not the richest, the wisest, the wittiest? So what? (quoted in Sean Covey, *Fourth Down and Life to Go*, 35)

Many of us feel insecure and compare ourselves with others when we attend church each Sunday. Other families seem so put together and in control, and we often get the impression that ours is *not* one of these families. This perspective can leave us feeling discontented and discouraged.

I remember being in sacrament meeting on one particular occasion when the young family in front of us was sitting

perfectly still without any books, crayons, or coloring note-
books to keep the kids occupied. Meanwhile, my kids were
taking turns crawling under the benches, dumping crayons all
over the floor, and teasing one another. *What's wrong with me
and my family?* I wondered silently. A short while later, I again
felt like a failure as I watched four perfectly dressed and
groomed children (in outfits made by their mother, I might
add) stand and play a beautifully prepared musical number—all
on stringed instruments. "I can barely get my kids to practice
their piano lessons a few times a week," I lamented.

One woman, a young mother of six boys, expressed to me
how exhausting Sundays are for her. To avoid being judged for
having "too many" children, she feels that her family has to look
perfect and behave properly each week to give the appearance of
being well-managed and under control. By the time she gets home
from church, however, she is utterly worn out from the effort of
maintaining this façade, which she concedes is far from reality.

It's safe to say that most women actually feel this same
way—whether it be because their children do not seem to be as
reverent as the children in the next pew, or because their family
doesn't seem quite as put together as the next-door neighbors. It
is also safe to say that if we base our feelings of self-worth on
any source other than the quality of our hearts and our identity
as daughters of God, we are basing it on a very shaky footing.

Elder Jeffrey R. Holland warned us to beware of "our
culture's obsession with comparing, competing, and never
feeling we are 'enough.'" This often flows, he pointed out, from
our own negative thinking about ourselves. "We see our own
faults, we speak—or at least think—critically of ourselves, and
before long that is how we see everyone and everything" ("The
Tongue of Angels," *Ensign*, May 2007, 17). This comparison
mentality is not only damaging to our self-esteem; when we
allow ourselves to feel inadequate, we are literally undervaluing
our divine worth.

All women have struggles of which we are often not aware.
Some struggle with infertility, others with wayward children, and
others with depression or a troubled marriage. Yet we typically

only see these women at their Sunday best, and if we were to judge them by appearances or compare our lot with theirs, we would truly end up with a distorted picture of reality. Thank heaven for the inspired counsel of our latter-day prophets and Apostles. Elder M. Russell Ballard reminded us:

> There is *no* one perfect way to be a good mother. Each situation is unique. Each mother has different challenges, different skills and abilities, and certainly different children. The choice is different and unique for each mother and each family. Many are able to be "full-time moms," at least during the most formative years of their children's lives, and many others would like to be. Some may have to work part- or full-time; some may work at home; some may divide their lives into periods of home and family and work. What matters is that a mother loves her children deeply and, in keeping with the devotion she has for God and her husband, prioritizes them above all else. ("Daughters of God," *Ensign*, May 2008, 108)

In this day and age, LDS mothers find themselves in nearly every circumstance imaginable. My hat goes off to the single mothers of the Church in particular; their capacity is enormous. To be able to perform well at a place of employment, hold a church calling, manage a household, and strive to raise righteous and responsible children *simultaneously* is an incredible feat and one that elicits my deepest respect and admiration. The working moms I know are as devoted to their families as are the mothers who are privileged to be at home full-time, and sometimes even more so, as they try to compensate for the time spent away from their children. One would be hard-pressed to find a more dedicated mother than my friend Barbara, who, as a single parent, has been compelled to work full-time while raising four of the brightest and most spiritually solid children I've ever met.

Heavenly Father knows these women's hearts—and He knows your heart. He knows of their righteous desires and how much they love their children, and He knows and accounts for their unique circumstances rather than comparing them to anyone else. And His is the only opinion that really counts.

Strengthening One Another in Our Efforts
As mothers, we're all in this together, and we need to strengthen and support one another in our efforts. Acknowledging the abilities and talents of others doesn't diminish us in any way; rather, their gifts serve to bless our lives and the lives of our children as we surround ourselves with and recognize other outstanding individuals. I am truly inspired by the LDS women I know—their capacities have been expanded by their experiences in the Church, by the way they are raising up families to the Lord, and by the teaching and leading they do both in church settings and at home.

I admire my friend Jody, who carefully prepared and sent a son and a daughter into the mission field within six months of each other, both armed with powerful testimonies and a family commitment to faithfulness. I marvel at the members of my book group, excellent women who are bright and articulate and capable, who could be pursuing any vocation they desire but have chosen motherhood as their first priority. I am amazed by the commitment and perspective of my sisters and sisters-in-law, who are such devoted and diligent mothers and are raising children who love the Lord. I applaud the young mother I overheard at a sacrament meeting I was visiting recently, who was telling her little boy about Jesus and the purpose of the sacrament. I turned around and told her, "You're a good mother. I've been listening to what you are teaching your son." We need to do more affirming and encouraging and less comparing and finding fault. There is a great reservoir of strength and sisterhood surrounding us—all we must do is choose to recognize, embrace, and encourage those around us rather than compare ourselves to one another.

I've never understood why critics who don't have a clue about our culture say that Mormon women are oppressed, subjugated, and held down. As a Mormon woman myself, I can testify that Mormon women are given enormous opportunities for growth and development. From the time we are little children, we are given occasion to speak, learn the doctrines of God's kingdom, and gain our own testimonies; as we grow older, we take on tremendous responsibilities as we teach, lead, serve, and literally run organizations. We find a bond of sisterhood in the Relief Society, and we are given visiting teachers to watch over us. If *anything*, we are empowered, strengthened, and encouraged to be our best selves and to contribute and make a difference in society.

Ann Romney is an example of an LDS woman who knows who she is and what she is about; her example gives those around her strength and encouragement. In a recent interview with *Utah Valley Magazine*, Ann was asked by a reporter if she was ever nervous giving speeches day after day as she would stump (provide support) for her husband, Mitt Romney, who was running for president of the United States. Ann replied, "I was never nervous. Not for a second. I'm more nervous showing my horse than speaking to a million people on TV."

When the reporter inquired as to what could have possibly prepared her for the intensity of the national spotlight, Ann responded, "Giving church talks. I've been Relief Society president, stake Young Women president. I've learned to run things and plan events and speak on a moment's notice. I've also been on a lot of boards. I've been on the United Way board with all of the big executives. I have a lot of confidence. And as far as the campaign, we felt like it was the right thing to do and we loved to be there" ("Would-Be First Lady Is a First-Rate Lady," *Utah Valley Magazine*, July/August 2008, 29–30).

Another example of an LDS mother who knows who she is and what she is about is Kathy Headlee Miner, who publicly acknowledges the opportunities for organization and leadership the Church provides its women. Kathy is the founder and director of *Mothers without Borders,* an international organization with the mission to relieve the suffering of children throughout the world. Recently, she spoke about her experiences serving on an international relief board organized after the tsunami hit Southeast Asia in 2005. Kathy was assigned to a committee along with delegates from the most prestigious relief organizations in the world, and before long she was appointed to be their spokesperson. Her fellow committee members were impressed with her organizational and leadership skills. They were curious about her prior experience, as she was an extremely capable, articulate, and accomplished person. They asked her, "What is your background?" She answered, "I'm a mother." Kathy realized that her experiences rearing a family and serving in the Church over a period of twenty-five years uniquely qualified her to lead an international relief effort.

I know that God knows and loves each of us perfectly and personally, and that He has a personal mission and an individual purpose for every one of His daughters. I also have a testimony that as we recognize, strengthen, and encourage those around us, we will bless many lives—our own included.

My mission as a mother is one I adopted from the purpose statement of the general Primary organization: "To teach [my] children the gospel of Jesus Christ and help them learn to live it." When we know that God loves us and that we can be instruments in His hands for good, and when we are filled with a sense of purpose and self-worth, we can be a powerful force for righteousness in our homes and communities. Sheri Dew, former counselor in the Relief Society general presidency, affirmed, "For though some would portray us [Latter-day Saint women] as dowdy and dominated rather than the dynamic, radiant women that we are, no woman is more persuasive, no woman has greater influence for good, no woman is a more vibrant instrument in the hands of the Lord than a woman of God who is thrilled to be who she is" ("Stand Tall and Stand Together," Conference Report, Oct. 2000).

OVERCOMING DISCONTENTMENT

> "Much is said about the drudgery and the confinement of the woman's role in the home. In the perspective of the gospel it is not so. There is divinity in each new life. There is challenge in creating the environment in which a child can grow and develop. There is partnership between the man and woman in building a family which can last throughout the eternities."
> —"Privileges and Responsibilities of Sisters," Spencer W. Kimball, *Ensign,* Nov. 1978, 105–106

Overcoming any feelings of discontentment in our lives is an important step in becoming fully content as mothers. As we seek assurance from our Heavenly Father that what we are doing as mothers is important and that the way we are raising our children is acceptable to Him, we will be supported and buoyed up with the knowledge that He is pleased with our efforts. Further, when we acquire an attitude of gratitude and adopt an eternal perspective about our circumstances, the Lord will help us understand why we are sometimes deprived of the blessings we seek. We will then come to feel truly content with who we are as mothers and satisfied with what we *have* been given.

Seeking Assurance

Many years ago, when my sister Cynthia was a young mother of small children, she had an experience that forever changed her paradigm about motherhood.

She was on vacation at Hebgen Lake, a favorite family getaway in Montana, and early one morning, while her kids were still asleep, she poured out her heart in prayer to Heavenly Father. She remembers:

It spilled out of me all at once—the frustrations and doubt, even anger, as I struggled to determine my own identity as a mother. I had three little preschoolers, and although they brought great joy to my life and I loved them with all of my heart, I wondered if the endless work I was doing was even important or worth the effort.

Aloud, I cried to God, almost resentfully, going through my routine: "All I do all day is get kids dressed and undressed, cook for and feed them, clean up a million messes, change diapers, care for every physical need, and then do it over and over again, every day. I didn't know this is what motherhood was all about. I'm tired of it! Is any of this even important? Will it make a difference in their lives?"

After I got it all out, I humbled myself and asked for help. I needed comfort and encouragement from my Heavenly Father if I was going to make it. And I needed it now. "Please help me," I prayed. "Help me see the purpose in all of this."

Suddenly, I felt the love of the Lord reach out to me from deep within my heart. First, He affirmed me: "You are a good mother. You're doing your best. You are giving your children care and love while they are little. They *need* you, and you are doing a good job." The message gave me much needed affirmation and comfort, but the next impression gave me peace. It came so strongly that I couldn't deny it was my answer from God: "Wherefore, be not weary in well-doing, for ye are laying the foundation of a great work. And out of small things proceedeth that which is great" (D&C 64:33).

I had loved this scripture for years, but now it was meant for me: a struggling, frustrated young mother with three children to care for. The Lord was telling me that I could not afford to be "weary" in my "well-doing"—the day-to-day nurturing of my children—which took up so much of my time. These early years would be a foundation for their lives; and from these "small things" would grow something "great."

Many years later, I now have a clearer perspective, and I've even experienced some "pay days," for which my husband and I are grateful. I've come to find that no service, love, or work on our children's behalf is ever wasted; rather, it serves as the foundation for their lives. The Lord's promise is being fulfilled right before my eyes. Although my children have normal struggles and problems as all children do, they are maturing into responsible adults who have testimonies, are serving missions, and are marrying in the temple. I now know that from the foundation of "small," but *significant,* things "proceedeth that which is great."

The axiom, "That which is most personal is most general" certainly applies here. Many mothers have experienced feelings similar to those Cynthia expressed. I know I have. But we may also find consolation in the personal revelation she received from the Lord, affirming the intrinsic value of what she is doing as a mother and the way she is raising her children, and apply it to our own situation. When Emma Smith was given a personal revelation through her husband, the Prophet Joseph Smith, the Lord broadened His message by concluding, "this is my voice unto all" (see D&C 25:16). Similarly, I believe that the Lord's reassurance to Cynthia applies to all diligent mothers. As we seek assurance and comfort from the Lord regarding our role as mothers, He will not fail us.

We can also find assurance through the teachings of prophets, Apostles, and leaders. Several years ago, I read the following excerpt from a speech given by Elder Neal A. Maxwell. Addressing his remarks to women at the 1983 BYU Women's Conference, he expressed perfectly the discontentment and lack of satisfaction we mothers often feel, and then he put into perspective the importance of what we mothers do:

> A very significant part of getting "settled" . . . consists of coming to terms with the common temptations and trials and the *seeming routine,* because *what seems commonplace seldom is. . . .*
>
> Occasionally, some individuals let the *seeming ordinariness* dampen their spirits. Though actually coping and growing, others lack the quiet, inner-soul satisfaction that can steady them, and are experiencing instead, a lingering sense that *there is something more important they should be doing . . .* as if what is quietly achieved in righteous individual living or in parenthood are not sufficiently spectacular." (*Church News,* Feb. 16, 2008, 2; emphasis added)

Elder Maxwell assures us that truly, despite the "seeming routine" and the "seeming ordinariness" of our lives, there is "[nothing] more important [we] should be doing" than fulfilling our role as mothers.

Assurance may also come to us from those whom we mother—our children. Casey Weierman, a friend in my ward, recently shared with me an experience she had. It happened on a day when she was bogged down with laundry, dirty dishes, and household chores—all of those mundane tasks that can be very discouraging to a mother. As she was helping her three-year-old son, Dax, get dressed, Casey began wondering, *Am I contributing anything to society? Am I making a difference in anyone's life? Does anyone even know I exist? Who am I? What am I worth?*

While Casey was silently pondering these questions, Dax looked up at his mother and said, "Mommy, I know who you are." Somewhat startled, because she had not verbalized these feelings, Casey responded curiously, "You do? Who am I, Dax?" His response was simply, "You are Heavenly Father's special helper."

At that moment, the Spirit testified to Casey that this was true. As we read in Matthew 21:16, "Out of the mouth of babes and sucklings thou hast perfected praise." The whisperings of the Spirit manifested to Casey that she was a daughter of God. It confirmed to her that Heavenly Father was aware of her situation, that He listened to, loved, and appreciated her. This same assurance can come to each of us as we strive to raise our children in the nurture of the Lord and seek His Spirit in our lives.

Cultivating an Attitude of Gratitude

There is a beautifully written memoir by Gerda Weissmann Klein entitled *All But My Life.* A classic in Holocaust literature, it tells the moving story of Gerda's three frightful years as a slave laborer in Nazi death camps, relates how she is forced to march from Germany to Czechoslovakia over a three-month period in the dead of winter, and tells of her miraculous liberation. (She ends up marrying her American liberator.)

Despite the horrific scene of brutality paraded before her eyes, Gerda discovers a basic goodness in humanity as she witnesses many acts of decency and kindness shown her by peasants and fellow inmates. During the death march, where one thousand girls begin and only one hundred and twenty survive, she thinks about prayer and how she has always thanked God for the many gifts He has bestowed upon her. She writes:

> I thought about my way of praying. It started in school [when I was about 12 years old] with a play about ancient Egypt. Each character uttered a prayer: the mighty Pharaoh prayed for

a victory, his opponent asked for his own
success, a sick man begged for health, the doctor
asked for people to be ill, and each prayer, clean
and swift, like a white bird, shot upward. In
Heaven, it met with the other prayer that had
asked for just the contrary. They turned against
each other in bloody battle, and usually both fell
back lifeless to the earth. A large number of girls
had taken part in that play. I thought I had a
beautiful role. I was a poor little boy, the son of
a fellah. My mother told me to pray, but I didn't
know how. I had no wishes, so I just looked at
the river that fertilized our field, at the warm
sun, at the ripe fruit in our garden, and I said,
"Thank you, God, for the warm sun, for the
blue Nile, for my father and mother," and my
little-boy prayer, like the others, sailed straight
up to the throne of God. Nobody defied my
prayer, and nobody else thanked the Maker.
They were all asking Him for things. He turned
His face upon the little barefoot boy. (185–186)

Likewise, instead of finding fault with life and always asking
why, we too must be willing to accept our circumstances with
an attitude of gratitude. President Ezra Taft Benson taught,
"The Prophet Joseph Smith is reported to have said at one time
that one of the greatest sins for which the Latter-day Saints
would be guilty would be the sin of ingratitude. I presume most
of us have not thought of that as a serious sin. There is a great
tendency for us in our prayers—in our pleadings with the
Lord—to ask for additional blessings. Sometimes I feel we need
to devote more of our prayers to expressions of gratitude and
thanksgiving for blessings already received" (*The Teachings of
Ezra Taft Benson*, 363).

It is a privilege and a blessing to be a mother, and it is a
calling that we must not esteem lightly. Thomas Paine, an

Englishman who adopted the cause of American independence from Great Britain as his own, wrote a stirring essay entitled "An American Crisis," which George Washington read to his troops on Christmas Eve of 1776 to boost their morale. Paine wrote, "[That which] we obtain too cheap, we esteem too lightly: 'tis dearness only that gives every thing its value. Heaven knows how to put a proper price upon its goods" (William Bennett, *Our Sacred Honor*, 36). In other words, Paine was declaring that independence was important and worth fighting for, an assertion that may be applied to motherhood as well. That which is worth having is often bought with a price: Just as we cherish our freedom as human beings, so must we hold motherhood equally as dear.

My sister was impressed with an excellent program entitled "Everyday Heroes" that was recently broadcast on public television. In this program, ordinary individuals were awarded for their extraordinary actions. One of the recipients of this award was a mother from the Midwest who had been in the direct line of a tornado. At the time, this woman's husband was on duty as a firefighter, and when he heard about the possibility that a tornado would be coming her way, he called to warn her. She was standing in the kitchen as they spoke on the telephone, and as she glanced out the window to see what he was talking about, she caught sight of the tornado coming directly toward her home—mere moments before it hit. She grabbed her two children and ran downstairs to the basement, where they huddled together as the tornado ripped through their home, destroying everything in its path. When the woman's neighbors found her after the storm passed, she was huddled over her children, with an arm around each of them. Miraculously, they were all alive, but the mother's back was broken, and she was left paralyzed.

This mother now uses a wheelchair and continues to painstakingly take care of her family. What impressed my sister the most about this woman was how content she was with her circumstances. She feels an enormous debt of gratitude to God for preserving her life and the lives of her children, and this gratitude has literally permeated her entire being. Instead of being embittered and angry, she is radiant and cheerful. She cherishes her life and family even more than before and deeply appreciates the beauties of the world around her. Since this life-altering event, she can't bear to miss a sunrise.

Isn't it revealing that often the people who are the most grateful and the most content are those who seemingly have the fewest reasons to be so? Recently, I have become acquainted with an outstanding member of the Church named Jason Hall. Although he is obviously not a mother, I have learned a great deal from him about what it means to be content and to cultivate an attitude of gratitude.

Jason has had two major accidents in his life. The first took place when he was a young man of fifteen, when he broke his neck jumping into Lake Powell in southern Utah; the second happened when he was a young adult, when he was driving his specially-equipped van on the freeway and his front tire popped, causing a devastating collision. In the car accident, he broke everything *but* his neck. He was in the hospital for thirteen months and literally had to relearn how to do everything—including breathe, which he said was the most difficult thing he had ever done in his life.

Despite these seemingly insurmountable obstacles, Jason has an attitude of gratitude unlike anyone I have ever seen. He has married a remarkable woman, served as the student body president of BYU, succeeded in the business world, and is now pursuing a career as a motivational speaker—all while struggling with severe physical limitations. When he spoke to the young women and young men of our ward at a recent youth conference, Jason expressed the concept that gratitude and discontentment cannot exist in the same person at the same time. He shared his insight that the key to contentment is to be grateful for all of the blessings we *do* have. He then bore testimony that He knows God is mindful of each of us, that He loves us, and that He will bless us with peace and happiness as we express gratitude for all of the blessings He has poured out upon us so abundantly. As I watched Jason sitting tall and strong in his wheelchair, bearing witness of the love of the Lord in his life, I felt an increase of gratitude for my own blessings—and trials.

I have learned for myself that discontentment is in actuality a form of ingratitude. Whether we are dissatisfied with the lack of or limited number of children we have been blessed with, or whether we struggle with the "seeming ordinariness" of our lives or deep-seated feelings of inadequacy as mothers, we ought to "be content with such things as [we] have" (Hebrews 13:5).

My two favorite scriptures on the subject are these:

"And in nothing doth man offend God, or against none is his wrath kindled, save those who *confess not his hand* in all things, and obey not his commandments" (D&C 59:21; emphasis added).

"Trust in the Lord with all thine heart; and lean not unto thine own understanding. In all thy ways *acknowledge Him,* and He shall direct thy paths" (Proverbs 3:5–6; emphasis added).

When we fail to confess the Lord's hand in all things and acknowledge His presence in our lives, we are guilty of the sin of ingratitude. However, as these scriptures affirm, when we trust in Him with all our hearts, acknowledge the abundance of His blessings in our lives, rely upon His wisdom and omnipotence and not upon our own limited understanding, He will *literally* direct our lives and paths. Heavenly Father promises in latter-day scripture that if we are humble, He will "lead [us] by the hand, and give [us] answer to [our] prayers" (D&C 112:10).

Elder Neal A. Maxwell put it this way:

> Before enjoying the harvests of righteous efforts, let us therefore first acknowledge God's hand. Otherwise, the rationalizations appear, and they include, "My power and the might of mine hand hath gotten me this wealth" (Deuteronomy 8:17). Or, we "vaunt" ourselves, as ancient Israel

would have done . . . by boasting that "mine own hand hath saved me" (Judges 7:2). Touting our own "hand" makes it doubly hard to confess God's hand in all things. ("Consecrate Thy Performance," *Ensign,* May 2002, 37)

Comprehending Deprivation

Why do we face the challenges we do in life? Why are blessings we are worthy to receive withheld from us at times? I have a niece who had righteously prepared to serve a mission her entire life, yet when the time came for her to turn in her mission papers, she was not allowed to go because of sudden poor health. Finally, after many months of medical care, she was able to go and serve as she had always desired.

My sister-in-law, a talented and beautiful person, has always wanted to marry and have children. Despite her righteous desires and efforts to keep the commandments, these blessings have been withheld from her at this time.

A close family member who has longed to be a mother has been unable to have children despite undergoing every medical procedure possible to get pregnant.

We would do well to look to Nephi's words. When asked by the Spirit if he understood the condescension of God, Nephi replied, "I know that he loveth his children; nevertheless, I do not know the meaning of all things" (1 Nephi 11:17). Similarly, we may not understand why we are sometimes deprived of the blessings we seek—particularly when they are the righteous desires of our hearts. Yet if we truly have faith and entrust ourselves to God's care, we too will be able to say with confidence that we know "[God] loveth his children," even though we may not comprehend why some of our righteous desires remain unfulfilled.

Several years ago, I had a conversation with my cousin Irene that I will never forget. We hadn't seen each other for quite a while, and so we were catching up on each other's lives. She asked me how many children I had, and I replied that my husband and I had three children, but I complained that we hadn't been able to have any more.

When I asked Irene about her family, she told me how she and her husband longed to be parents, how they would love to have a big family, but after years of infertility treatment and heartache, they had finally accepted that they would never be able to bear children of their own.

As I listened to Irene speak with such acceptance of the Lord's will, I felt reprimanded by my conscience through Alma's words: "*I ought to be content* with the things which the Lord hath allotted unto me" (Alma 29:3; emphasis added).

Since that conversation with Irene many years ago, my husband and I have been blessed with two more children, both born while we were living in Hawaii: Colin Kamakana, whose middle name means "gift from God" in Hawaiian; and Megan Michelle, who is the light of our lives. Irene and her husband, Paul, have since adopted *eight* beautiful children. Behind every adoption is a miraculous and spiritually uplifting account of how each child came into their home.

A short time ago, a dear friend wrote to me about her inability to become pregnant again after having her first baby a few years earlier. She shared, "The difficult challenge of becoming pregnant is one of the reasons that I'm so happy to be home with my little girl. To think that I have her at all sometimes causes me to tear up and thank the Lord. She is my miracle child. But I still struggle with some of the same feelings I had before giving birth to her. I thought I'd overcome those feelings, but sometimes they creep back in. I feel jealous of those who can plan the number and/or timing of their children. I struggle with those women who are annoyed at being pregnant, even though it was a planned thing for them, and who complain that their babies aren't coming in the right month. One pregnant woman I know was bothered that her baby was due in May instead of in March, and said she would absolutely die if it wasn't a girl and didn't have lots of hair. It seemed like such a petty complaint to someone like me who is just longing to have a baby. Sometimes I don't think people can even comprehend how truly blessed they are."

I love the wise perspective Elder Neal A. Maxwell offers to those who, like my friend, anxiously await certain blessings: "Some deprivations are but delayed blessings, which, if endured well, constitute the readying of reservoirs into which a generous God will pour 'all that He hath.' Indeed, it will be the Malachi measure: 'There shall not be room enough to receive it'" (*We Will Prove Them Herewith*, 28–29).

Gay Jones, a woman in my stake, is an example of someone who has experienced this "Malachi measure" in her own life. Although deprived of marriage and motherhood for most of her adult years, Gay was determined to live a rich, full life. She studied law and created a meaningful career, becoming the general counsel to the Utah legislature.

Knowing that God was mindful of her and that she had not been forgotten, she reached out for companionship to her five siblings and twenty-five nieces and nephews. When possible, she attended their recitals, plays, baptisms, and other special events. She vacationed with a niece and her family in Hawaii, Nauvoo, Yellowstone, and Disneyland. As a single sister, she had tremendous "mothering" experiences. These relationships became very important in her life. Not only did she support and give love to her extended family, but she received great love and support in return. Gay took care of her mother for the last six years of her mother's life, and during the viewing and funeral, Gay's family literally surrounded her with their physical presence, never allowing her to be without a companion, which helped to sustain her through her grief.

Then, at age fifty-three, Gay met and married a widower who had six grown children and sixteen grandchildren. Understanding that her new husband's children might have a difficult time accepting her right away, she focused on winning over the grand-children. Because of her substantial experience with her nieces and nephews, she already had a great love for and understanding of children, so it was natural for Gay to play chess, swim, enjoy movies, ski, and simply *play* with these grandchildren. As a result, they have become her friends—as have her stepchildren. One of the most thrilling moments Gay has experienced as a new grandmother was when, upon seeing Gay on a Webcam over the Internet, her three-year-old granddaughter screamed with excitement, "It's Grandma! It's Grandma!"

Although her life has not turned out the way she had envisioned, in retrospect, Gay knows that God had a design for her life and that it is coming together according to His plan. The deprivation she experienced was like "the readying of a well" into which the Lord eventually poured "all that He hath."

Speaking of women who have been deprived of some blessings in life, Patricia Holland promises in her book, *A Quiet Heart:*

> Believe me when I tell you that God is a God of goodness, mercy, and justice. Ultimately, he cannot treat his righteous children differently. Whatever blessings you have gone without will be made up to you in divine and glorious fashion. I give you every assurance, they will be made up to you to the point where you will not be confident that God treated you fairly but embarrassed that he treated you so very generously. (30–31)

God knows how to give good gifts to His children. As a loving Father, He will not give His child a stone if He is asked for bread. Always, the gifts are given in His own due time; if we are required to wait for some blessings, or even do without some blessings here on earth, we can look forward in faith, knowing that our righteous desires *will* be fulfilled. Eventually, He will provide greater things than we can even imagine, for, as He foretold, "Since the beginning of the world men have not heard, nor perceived by the ear, neither hath the eye seen, O God, beside thee, what he hath prepared for him *that waiteth for him*" (Isaiah 64:4; emphasis added).

LEARNING TO BE CONTENT

Paul to the Philippians: "Not that I speak in respect of want:
for I have learned, in whatsoever state I am, therewith to be
content."

—Philippians 4:11

As mothers, we can glean much from the Apostle Paul's perspective that in "whatsoever state" he found himself, he "learned . . .
to be content." At times, we may not be able to control the
circumstances in which we find ourselves, but we *can* control
the way we react to those circumstances. Learning to be content
comes more easily to a mother when she recognizes that the key
to happiness is obedience to God, makes peace with the "invisibility" of her efforts, comes to appreciate the "sacred nature of
family work," learns to strengthen her identity through
moments of solitude, and develops a rich private life.

Discovering That "The Only Way to Be Happy Is to Be Obedient"
Patricia Holland, wife of Elder Jeffrey R. Holland of the Quorum
of the Twelve Apostles, tells of an experience she had as a young
woman, that eternally defined for her how to find happiness and
peace. She was living away from home for the summer, working in
Salt Lake City with some girls her own age. She speaks of the
enjoyable experiences the girls had together that summer but then
tells of a period of time when feelings of despondency and
discouragement invaded their apartment—so much so that
Patricia felt led to fast and pray about how to be happy and to find
the peace, security, and confidence that every person needs.

On the evening of her fast, Patricia's friends persuaded her
to go to a movie with them, and on the way the girls stopped to

buy some snacks at the grocery store. While there, they met Elder Elray Christiansen, an assistant to the Quorum of the Twelve Apostles, who showed an interest in them and learned each girl's name. "Just before Elder Christiansen got ready to leave," recalls Patricia, "he paused, looked right at me, and said, 'Pat, the only way to be happy is to be obedient.'

"To have my prayers answered so directly was a turning point in my life," Sister Holland remembers. "I realized right then and there that truly the greatest thing I could cling to, the only way to be confident and happy, is to be obedient and live by the Spirit" (Ardeth G. Kapp, "'The Only Way to Be Happy': Pat Holland," *New Era,* Apr. 1981, 40).

This principle is taught countless times throughout the scriptures. My favorite explanation of how to obtain true happiness is found in King Benjamin's great address to his people: "And moreover, I would desire that ye should consider on the blessed and *happy* state of those that keep the commandments of God. For behold, they are blessed in all things, both temporal and spiritual; and if they hold out faithful to the end they are received into heaven, that thereby they may dwell with God in a state of never-ending *happiness*" (Mosiah 2:41; emphasis added).

Happiness, peace, and contentment are the natural consequences of obedience. In a revelation given through Joseph Smith the Prophet, the Lord confirmed: "But learn that he who *doeth the works of righteousness* shall receive his reward, even *peace* in this world, and eternal life in the world to come" (D&C 59:23; emphasis added).

Having faith, obediently keeping the commandments, and acknowledging God's hand in all things places us in an eternal spiral that continues upward and perpetuates itself. When we have faith that God will answer our prayers and bless us, act upon that faith by following Him and keeping His commandments, and then immediately confess His hand in our lives and acknowledge His blessings, our faith will grow into a sure knowledge and become even stronger. We will then have an even greater desire to follow Him and to do His will, which will afford us an even deeper gratitude to Him for all of the blessings He has so abundantly poured out upon us, and so on, and so on.

Cycle of Spiritual Growth

Faith
"And now, I, Moroni, would speak somewhat concerning these things; I would show unto the world that faith is things which are hoped for and not seen; wherefore, dispute not because ye see not, for ye receive no witness until after the trial of your faith."

—Ether 12:6

Acknowledge God's Hand in All Things/Collect Evidences
"In all thy ways acknowledge him and he shall direct thy paths."

—Proverbs 3:6)

Obedience/Action
"Be ye doers of the word and not hearers only."

—James 1:22)

Blessings
"All that he requires of you is to keep his commandments . . . therefore, if ye do keep his commandments he doth bless you and prosper you."

—Mosiah 2:22

Elder Bruce R. McConkie says of this process of faith, obedience, and blessings: "Faith is a gift of God bestowed as a reward for personal righteousness. It is always given when right-eousness is present, and the greater the measure of obedience to God's laws the greater will be the endowment of faith" (*Mormon Doctrine,* 2nd ed. [1966], 264). I have also been enlightened by the experience Elder McConkie's brother Oscar had while he was serving as a missionary in California. Oscar remembers that he had many challenges before him, and on one particular occa-sion, he prayed to God that he might be blessed with faith like unto Enoch and Elijah to enable him to accomplish his work. Instructively, the voice of the Spirit revealed to him, "Enoch and Elijah obtained their faith through righteousness" (Conference Report, Oct. 1952, 56–57). Without a doubt, the personal righteousness that results from obedience can be a powerful source of inner strength through which our faith may grow and through which we may find happiness.

Before I left on my mission to Ireland, I took an extremely helpful missionary preparation class from an outstanding teacher, Con Gottfredson, at BYU. Brother Gottfredson inspired the members of his class to "collect evidences" that we would succeed in our missionary work. He taught us to search out God's promises throughout the scriptures that were applic-able to missionary work, such as, "I will go before your face. I will be on your right hand and on your left, and my Spirit shall be in your hearts, and mine angels round about you, to bear you up" (D&C 84:88); and, "Behold, I will go before you and be your rearward; and I will be in your midst, and you shall not be confounded" (D&C 49:27); and, "Yea, I will open the hearts of the people, and they will receive you" (D&C 31:7).

Then he suggested that we needed to develop faith that God would fulfill these promises to His missionaries. He promised that as we exercised faith and lived worthy of those promises, we would be blessed according to our righteous desires—and our faith would grow.

I took his suggestions to heart and have since developed an overwhelming "collection of evidences" that God truly does fulfill His promises to me as I am obedient. And as my journal-keeping sister has pointed out, by *recording* these evidences, I have acquired a personal "book of revelation" as I recognize the pattern of God's hand in my life.

Taking Care of the Invisible
In her book *Mitten Strings for God,* Katrina Kenison discusses a quotation by Peggy O'Mara, author of *The Way Back Home* and editor of *Mothering* magazine: "[O'Mara states that] 'All that is really important is invisible: love, God, air.' Mothers who try to put families first, [O'Mara] suggests, are the nobility of today, because they take care of the invisible" (168–169).

Anne Morrow Lindbergh, in *Gift from the Sea,* concurs with this notion: "We do not see the results of our giving as concretely as man does in his work. In the job of home-keeping there is no raise from the boss, and seldom praise from others to show us we have hit the mark. Except for the child, woman's creation is so often invisible" (40).

I too have realized that an enormous chunk of my day is spent "taking care of the invisible." Yesterday, that meant listening to my nine-year-old, Megan, read *Bread and Jam for Frances* for the fifteenth time. Last night it meant building a topical map of Utah, complete with mountains, rivers, and lakes, entirely out of cupcakes and frosting, with my sixteen-year-old, Christine. This morning it meant helping my eleven-year-old, Colin, make his bed and practice his piano. These simple everyday gestures—when carried out with love and attention—can be deeply significant in the life of a child. These "invisible" actions can also afford us a deep sense of content-ment as we realize their significance to our loved ones and learn that they are not invisible in the eyes of God.

Katrina Kenison shares Mother Teresa's insight on the subject: "We must not think that our love has to be extraordi-nary. But we do need to love without getting tired. How does a lamp burn? Through the continuous input of small drops of oil. These drops are the small things of daily life: faithfulness, small words of kindness, a thought for others, our way of being quiet, of looking, of speaking, and of acting. They are the true drops of love that keep our lives and our relationships burning like a lively flame" (*Mitten Strings for God*, 173). As mothers, we need to enjoy the "little" things in life; for one day we may look back and realize that they *were* the "big" things.

Appreciating the Sacred Nature of Family Work

Several years ago, my parents sent each of their children an article by Kathleen Bahr, an associate professor at BYU, entitled, "The Sacred Nature of Everyday Work." Since then, I've had the privilege of reading more from Sister Bahr and have heard her speak on this subject at BYU Education Week. In short, her teachings have transformed my paradigm about the everyday work I do within my home, and I have been profoundly changed by her insights.

Sister Bahr points out that the Savior taught that our willingness to perform life-sustaining tasks for one another will actually separate the sheep from the goats at the time of judgment (see Matthew 25:31–33). Let's look at the following oft-quoted scripture, a statement made by the Savior, through a unique perspective—that of a mother:

> For I was an hungered, and ye gave me meat: I was thirsty and ye gave me drink: I was a stranger, and ye took me in:
>
> Naked, and ye clothed me: I was sick, and ye visited me: I was in prison, and ye came unto me.
>
> Then shall the righteous answer him, saying, Lord, when saw we thee an hungered, and fed thee? or thirsty, and gave thee drink?
>
> When saw we thee a stranger, and took thee in? or naked and clothed thee?
>
> Or when saw we thee sick, or in prison, and came unto thee?

> And the King shall answer and say unto
> them, Verily I say unto you, Inasmuch as ye
> have done it unto one of the least of these my
> brethren, ye have done it unto me. (Matthew
> 25:35–40)

In other words, the saving work that will determine where *we* sit, at the Savior's right hand or left, is the humble work of feeding, clothing, and caring for our children! Sister Bahr further queries, "In a world that rewards and glorifies the work we do for the masses before the eyes of all men, where do we feed, clothe, and care for 'the least of Christ's brothers and sisters?' Perhaps it is as simple and as meaningful as noting the needs of our parents, our siblings, and our children in our own homes" (188).

"Work is love made visible," an old proverb says. I think of these words as I scrub the breakfast dishes after my kids troop out the door; watch my young-adult son, Covey, push the lawn mower; or entrust Saturday's cleaning to my teenaged daughter, Hannah. As author Katrina Kenison has so eloquently stated, "Here we are, working together for the good of all, enlivened by our efforts, bringing grace to our home" (*Mitten Strings for God*, 148).

However, family work—the necessary, hands-on labor of sustaining life—has become the work that no one wants to do. We do well to remember that in every dispensation of time, in every walk of life, people need to be fed, clothed, sheltered, and nurtured. Family work is universal, and it can bind us to one another by providing endless opportunities to fill the needs of others.

Kathleen Bahr insists that there is a sacred nature to everyday work:

> [Our] daily toiling is in honor of life itself. After
> all, isn't this temporal work of tending to the
> necessary and routine currents of daily life,

whether for our families or for our neighbors, the work we really came to Earth to do? By this humble service—this washing of one another's feet—we sacrifice our pride and invite God to wash our own souls from sin. Indeed, such work embodies within it the condescension of the Savior himself. It is nothing less than doing unto Christ, by serving the least of our brethren, what He has already done for us. ("Family Work," *BYU Magazine,* Spring 2000, 30)

Sister Bahr also points out that although our larger culture portrays everyday family work as mindless and devoid of meaning, tasks that can be done with minimal concentration, such as washing dishes and folding clothes, free up our minds and spirits to attend to things that matter most: relationships and mental and spiritual renewal. While working side by side with our children, we are able to listen, talk, sing, and tell stories. Unlike play, which requires mental energy, family work is often menial, inviting intimate conversation between a parent and child. We can work without concentrating on the task at hand, allowing us to focus our attentions completely on the child.

My aunt Toni has taught second grade for thirty years now. She has learned through experience as well as through professional training that when a teacher talks to a student about something important, the two should sit side by side rather than face to face. When sitting side by side, students feel less intimidated and more on the same level as the teacher. I've noticed that this applies to parents and children as well. The other day, my husband and I were working side by side with our oldest son as we cleaned the kitchen, and our conversation flowed much more freely and naturally than it had the night before when we were trying to draw him out, face to face, about what was going on in his life.

A sense of contentment and accomplishment can also be gleaned when working alone on so-called "menial" tasks. In such an environment, a mother's mind is free to meditate, ponder, and store up knowledge. I remember my mother going about her household responsibilities while listening to the scriptures on tape. I likewise get many of my books "read" for my monthly book group as I listen while I work. Listening to Charles Dickens' *David Copperfield* on CD over the course of a few weeks as I worked was an enlightening experience for me. Since I didn't have to concentrate on the tasks, my spirit was free to imagine, and my mind was ready to learn. As a mother, some of the times I have felt the Spirit the strongest, felt the greatest sense of contentment, and received the greatest insights, have been while going about my everyday work.

As Delbert L. Stapley acknowledged, "Good habits are developed in the workshop of our daily lives. It is not in the great moments of test and trial that character is built. That is only when it is displayed. The habits that direct our lives and form our character are fashioned in the often uneventful, commonplace routine of life" (*Ensign,* Nov. 1974, 20).

However, mothers often become discouraged by these ordinary routines of daily life. Without the proper perspective, the demands of crying children, the drudgery of housework, and the nagging feeling that there is more to life than what we are experiencing can lead to discontentment and unhappiness.

But with the proper perspective, we can realize that that which *seems* commonplace seldom is. As Joseph F. Smith stated:

> We should never be discouraged in those daily tasks which God has ordained to the common lot of man. Each day's labor should be undertaken in a joyous spirit and with the thought and conviction that our happiness and eternal welfare depend upon doing well that which we ought to do, that which God has made it our duty to do. Many are unhappy because they imagine that they should be doing something unusual or something phenomenal. . . . Let us

not be trying to substitute an artificial life for the true one. [She] is truly happy who can see and appreciate the beauty with which God has ordained the commonplace things of life." (Joseph F. Smith, *Gospel Doctrine*, 285–286)

Strengthening Our Identities through Solitude
As members of the Church, we have been encouraged by our leaders to form habits of personal, private worship, such as feasting daily upon the scriptures, deep and meaningful prayer, meditation, regular temple attendance, and studying inspiring literature. In addition to pursuing other worthwhile goals, these habits can help an LDS mother feel content with who she is and who she is becoming by affording her moments of solitude in which she may process, ponder, learn, and grow. As Katrina Kenison writes, "I remind myself that it is . . . who I *am* as a human being that will make a deep and lasting impression on my children. I can bring peace [contentment] to my children only when I possess it myself" (*Mitten Strings for God,* 160).

In her book *Spiritually Centered Motherhood,* LDS author Sherrie Johnson likewise suggests that a woman must be content with herself before she can ever become a spiritually centered mother. "A woman who is not at peace with herself, who has never learned who she is or where she is going, who has not mastered herself, and who does not like herself cannot effectively teach her children because of her own distress [discontentment]" (20).

Ultimately, we teach what we are. The familiar expression rings true: "I cannot hear what you *say* because what you *are* rings so loudly in my ears."

From my perspective, the best way for a woman to replenish herself and ultimately find contentment is through moments of solitude in which she is able to be inwardly attentive. A mother especially needs solitude in order to detect and refresh her true identity and mission. Elder Richard G. Scott counsels, "Find a retreat of peace and quiet where you can ponder and let the

Lord establish the direction of your life. Each of us needs to periodically check our bearings and confirm that we are on course" ("First Things First," *Ensign,* May 2001, 9).

After twenty years of being a mother, my children are all in school now. I cried for the first week, missing them and mourning the loss of having a preschooler at home. After that initial week, however, I became giddy at the prospect of having a little more private time. For the first time in many years, I no longer have to lock myself in the bathroom to be alone during the day. (Even then, the kids would pound on the door, demanding to be let in.) I have found that when I set aside time to study the scriptures and pray, reflect upon and strengthen my testimony of the restored gospel of Jesus Christ, and gain a strong sense of identity and purpose, I can more confidently guide my life and the lives of my children.

But a mother need not wait until all her children are in school to find these moments of solitude and self-reflection. My sister Colleen, a mother of six children, including two preschoolers, enjoys her moments of solitude at night after the kids have gone to bed. Since the age of fourteen, she has been an avid journal writer and has to date filled seventy volumes. To take some alone time to read her scriptures and write in her journal every day has become a necessity for her and is her way of being "inwardly attentive." Her journal allows her to find out what she thinks, assess the day, and reaffirm her priorities. I've noticed that as she has done this, Colleen has developed a tremendous respect for language, and she is careful with her words and measured in her conversations. She has become a better person and a better mother because of her commitment to daily solitude.

My stake Relief Society president, Teresa Christensen, learned this principle in a profound way. She distinctly remembers the moment when, as a young mother of three small children, she was lying on the floor of her living room with her children while driving match box cars around an imaginary track and feeling terribly unfulfilled. Then the thought came to her mind: *Whate'er thou art act well thy part,* the motto that President David O' McKay had come across during his mission to Scotland (see Elaine S. Dalton, "He Knows You by Name," *Ensign,* May 2005, 109).

As Teresa continued driving those cars around and around, reflecting upon that statement, a light went on in her head. *I am a mother!* she realized. *And I want to 'act well my part.' If my children are going to grow up as happy, successful adults and become people whose lives center around the gospel and service to others, it is up to me to influence them in these directions. If this is what I want, I must get to work!*

Teresa began to throw herself into motherhood. Among other things, she set up family schedules and instituted practices that she felt would help her children grow into responsible and capable individuals. Life was busy as her family grew from three children to nine. She felt energized about the routines she had established; she had a purpose and a focus. But still, she sensed that something was lacking.

One day, while reading a statement by President Ezra Taft Benson, Teresa discovered what it was that she was missing. President Benson pointed out the number of resources that had been put into place to help individuals and families: new additions of the scriptures, more temples conveniently located to the membership of the Church, the consolidated meeting schedule, new family home evening manuals, a new hymnal. Then he admonished, "We have received much help. We don't need changed programs now as much as we need changed people!" ("Cleansing the Inner Vessel," *Ensign,* May 1986, 4–7).

It was then that Teresa recognized that while she had put a lot of energy into creating "programs" for her family, so to speak, she personally felt stagnant. She asked herself, *Has the gospel really sunk deep into* my *heart? Do I really know who* I *am and what that means? Do I really know and believe the things* I've *been taught all of my life?* She says, "I began to realize that only when I gained a better understanding and commitment to *my* purpose and mission on earth, would I truly understand the purpose and focus of my mothering. I was enjoying the comforts of Zion, but had become distracted with all of the 'good things,' rather than the 'essential ones.' Although I was 'training up my children in the way *they* should go,' I also needed to be working on those same things for myself."

Teresa went to the Lord in fasting and prayer, knowing that she needed His help. Revelation came in powerful and specific ways. She felt inspired that she must also "fill her own lamp" (see the parable of the ten virgins in Matthew 25) while endeavoring to teach her family. Teresa resolved to get up early every morning to study her scriptures, exercise, have a meaningful prayer, shower, and get ready for the day before her children arose and her busy family routine began. She started to fast often and attend the temple regularly so that she could more fully feel the Spirit of the Lord in her life. Teresa learned that part of "acting well her part" meant taking care of her needs as well as her family's.

With the Lord's help, Teresa has done these things through the years as she has raised her family. She is now in the "empty nester" phase of life and can testify that by regularly paying the price to make time for daily renewal, her testimony of the significance of motherhood has been enhanced, her personal revelation has increased, and her gospel teachings to her family have had more spiritual depth and power. Due to her concerted efforts to consistently "fill her own lamp," Teresa has found great meaning and fulfillment in her life—and in her mothering. She feels whole and complete as an individual and as a mother.

An Indian businessman who greatly admired Mother Teresa of Calcutta and desired to help her in her work printed, at her request, five lines on some yellow "business cards" that clearly explained the direction of her work. She freely offered these cards to people to describe the "simple path" she followed. The path is composed of five essential steps:

The Simple Path
The fruit of silence is
PRAYER.
The fruit of prayer is
FAITH.
The fruit of faith is
LOVE.
The fruit of love is
SERVICE.
The fruit of service is
PEACE.

I find it very interesting that this simple path begins with *silence* (solitude) and ends with *peace* (contentment), and that in between are found actions: *prayer, faith, love,* and *service.* As we make the effort to be still, to prayerfully reflect upon our lives and missions, and to make deep commitments with the Lord, we renew our resolution to love and serve our families and our fellow men. In solitude, we gain a greater understanding not only of who *we* are, but also of who *God* is. As the psalmist wrote, "Be still, and know that I am God" (Psalm 46:10).

Throughout the gospels, we read that Christ often "withdrew himself" into a solitary place to pray, fast, and ponder His divine mission (see Matthew 14:23; Mark 1:35; Luke 4:42). At one point, when the Savior is discovered by his Apostles and a multitude of followers, one of them observes, "[Master], this is a solitary place" (JST, Mark 6:35). Those moments of solitude, which the Savior purposely sought out, likely helped give Him the resolve, the power, and the strength to fully carry out His Father's will and to finish His mission here on earth.

In the same vein, a mother must set aside some time each day for contemplation, study, and prayer in order to maintain her core, renew her spirit, and gain the strength and resolve to fully carry out the Father's will for her life.

I have found that for *me,* the key to setting aside moments of solitude doesn't rely on keeping a particular schedule or established time-table, although such routines can assist in making sure these moments happen every day; rather, I have found that it is the *quality* and *consistency* of these actions that is the key. Through the years, the time of my personal worship has varied depending on the stage of life I've been in. I've tried setting aside time first thing in the morning, the last thing at night, or even in the middle of the day, when my toddlers were napping. But none of this has seemed to matter as much as whether I approach the scriptures *prayerfully* and *consistently,* "with a sincere heart, with real intent, having faith in Christ" (Mor. 10:4). When, as Moroni encourages, I have approached my personal worship literally hungering and thirsting after the things of the Spirit, I have been filled.

What President Spencer W. Kimball says of personal study and growth is true: "I find that when I get *casual* in my relation-ships with divinity and when it seems that no divine ear is listening and no divine voice is speaking that I am far, far away. *If I immerse myself in the scriptures* the distance narrows and the spirituality returns" (*Teachings of Presidents of the Church: Spencer W. Kimball* [2006], 67; emphasis added).

I am astounded by the goodness and graciousness of God. Even when we so much as *attempt* to reach out to Him, He pours out His Spirit abundantly upon us. He desires so much to bless us. I love the image presented in the book of Revelation: "Behold, I stand at the door, and knock: if any man hear my voice, and open the door, I will come in to him, and will sup with him, and he with me" (Rev. 3:20). He is literally *waiting* for us to draw closer to Him; we only need to listen for His voice, open the door, and *allow* Him to come into our lives.

Developing a Rich Private Life
There is an incredible little book written in 1938 by the prolific writer Brenda Ueland, entitled, *If You Want to Write: A Book about Art, Independence, and Spirit.* My favorite chapter is called, "Why women who do too much housework should neglect it for their writing." Brenda's point is that every day, in

addition to carrying out our homemaking duties, we women need to tap into our imaginations, whether it be through writing, art, music, gardening, or anything that we love and want to do or make. She asserts that the best way to help your family progress in any aspect of life is to progress yourself—to be a fine and shining example of what you want them to become.

> For to teach, encourage, cheer up, console, amuse, stimulate or advise a husband or children or friends, *you have to be something yourself.* And how to be something yourself? Only by working hard and with gumption at something you love and care for and think is important.
>
> So if you want your children to be musicians, then work at music yourself, seriously and with all your intelligence. If you want them to be scholars, study hard yourself. If you want them to be honest, be honest yourself. And so it goes.
>
> And that is why I would say to the worn and hectored mothers who longed to write and could find not a minute for it: If you would shut your door against the children for an hour a day and say: "Mother is working on her five-act tragedy in blank verse!" you would be surprised how they would respect you. They would probably all become playwrights. (100; emphasis added)

Cultivating a rich private life is a necessity for a mother. "To be something yourself" empowers a woman to influence for good all those with whom she associates. I am grateful for a husband who, due to his unselfish devotion and desire to make me happy, has encouraged and made time for me to pursue my interests in reading, writing, teaching, and community service. (Not all at once, mind you.) My being caught up in writing this book over the past few years has been a spiritually rich and rewarding experience for our whole family, largely because it has been a growing experience for me as a mother.

As I strive to cultivate a rich private life, I am careful to limit my involvement outside of the home, knowing how easy it is "to forget the fundamental purpose of life," as Elder Richard G. Scott has warned. "Satan has a powerful tool to use against good people. It is distraction. He would have good people fill life with 'good things' so there is no room for the essential ones" ("First Things First," *Ensign,* May 2001, 7). Keeping this crucial caveat in mind, I am convinced that a woman's efforts to become a better, more well-rounded person will serve to help her be a more influential mother.

I love the philosophies of the renowned musician and teacher Dr. Shinichi Suzuki. Two of our children are learning his approach in their study of flute and violin. He writes, "The real essence of art turned out to be not something high up and far off—it was right inside my ordinary, daily self—If a musician wants to become a finer artist, he must first become a finer person" (SAU Family Newsletter, Fall 2006). We could easily substitute the word *mother* into this last line: If a woman wants to become a finer mother, she must first become a finer person.

Despite the demands of raising nine children, my mother has always enjoyed a rich private life. In addition to her habits of personal worship, she was constantly reading: classical literature, biographies of notable people, American history, and politics. She learned about art history on her own, and when she had the opportunity to travel with my dad on business, she would always visit the famous art museums and historical sites nearby. When she returned home from her travels armed with maps, pamphlets, postcards, playbills, photos, and art books, she would teach us what she'd learned. Her enthusiasm was contagious, and we learned to love history, art, theater, culture, and great literature— all from her example.

Lee Benson wrote a column in the *Deseret News* about a woman who has created a rich private life and uses her time wisely, while at the same time juggling motherhood. On the surface, Benson explains, Lindsey Dunkley appears to be a full-time mother of three, but on the sly, she is also a runner. In high school, Lindsey was a multiple-state track champion; and at BYU, she continued her winning ways as an all-American distance runner in both cross country and track. When she got married and became a mom, Lindsey thought she'd have to abandon her running aspirations for early-morning feedings and late-night changings. Not wanting her running to conflict with her role as wife and mother, yet realizing that being a runner is a large part of who she is, Lindsey bought a treadmill and put it in her basement.

Every day, at 6:00 A.M., after her husband has left for work and her children are still asleep, Lindsey retreats to her basement and runs six-minute miles (her treadmill won't go any faster) for about forty minutes. She's exercised, showered, and dressed for the day by 8:30 A.M.

Lindsey realizes that she's probably blown her cover, however, as her "treadmill training" has helped her win all four 5K races she's entered this year out of fields of hundreds. She isn't too concerned, however; she knows that the example she is setting for her children will encourage them to pursue their own talents and endeavors.

Notwithstanding the challenges of being a "weekend warrior" with three small children to care for, Lindsey wouldn't trade her circumstances for anything. "I was watching the Olympic trials last month," she said. "The girls going to Beijing, they're all my age. I used to run against them. I was thinking about that, and then I thought, I'll take my family. I would be very empty without them." Her family—and her treadmill, of course ("Treadmill Lets Mother of 3 Stay in Race," July 16, 2008).

Developing a rich private life can include our children as well. In fact, our example of using time wisely, developing our talents, and prioritizing can have a very positive effect on their lives. My sister Colleen, whom I referred to earlier in this chapter, told me of an experience related to this concept that she had not long ago with her twelve-year-old son, Matthew. As they were going over the tasks that needed to be completed that day, Colleen reminded Matthew that he hadn't done his twenty minutes of reading yet. Matthew, wanting to be finished so that he could play with a friend, replied rather irritatedly, "Why do you always make *me* read? Why don't *you* ever read?" Colleen was shocked. Not only did she have a master's degree in English literature, but she was *constantly* reading to keep up with the two book clubs to which she belonged. She realized, however, that her children rarely saw her read because she did so after they were in bed. Matthew had no idea how much she valued reading. Because of this, Colleen has decided to share the things she loves *with* her children and to do those activities together.

I recently learned about two sisters who are doing just that. Emily McPhie and Cassandra Barney, daughters of the famed fantasy artist and longtime BYU professor James C. Christensen, have successfully established themselves as gallery artists. While they were growing up, they remember their father retreating to his art studio with a stern warning to his five children that he was not to be disturbed. "Art was Dad's work, and while it was intriguing, it was sacred, and we respected that," says Cassandra Barney (Charlene Renberg Winters, "The Art of Family," *BYU Magazine,* Spring 2007, 33).

However, privacy while painting has not been an option for either Emily or Cassandra, as each is now a mother of three, and neither wants to exclude her children. For the Christensen sisters, motherhood is their top priority, and they have both made a conscious decision to draw their children into their home studios.

"Even when I was working on my master's degree, my space included [my children's] desk with all the paints, markers, pencils, and other art tools they wanted," Cassandra remembers. "We refer to it as 'our studio.' It has become such a part of our lives that when my daughter Sunshine went to play at a friend's home, she came home incredulous because they didn't have an art studio" (ibid., 33–34).

Like her sister, Emily works in her home studio with her children by her side. "Half my studio is their table with their drawers filled with paper and supplies," she says. "This keeps them busy while I keep painting." Even Emily and Cassandra's father, James Christensen, has allowed his painting habits to evolve to include painting space for a second artist—either a daughter or a grandchild (ibid., 35).

My dear friend Karen Hughes is another mother with a passion. When Karen was growing up, she excelled as a violinist and had opportunities to play with symphonies, in recording studios, and at private concerts. She loved playing the violin— in large part, it defined who she was—and she determined that when she became a mother she would cultivate this ardor for classical music and performing in her family. And she has.

Karen's sixteen-year-old daughter, Andrea, was recently selected as one of the Utah Symphony's "Salute to Youth" finalists, qualifying her, along with five other outstanding Utah teens, for the honor of performing with the orchestra. Watching her daughter perform with the Utah Symphony in all of her radiance was one of the highlights of Karen's life. She acknowledges, "She's passed me up." And she couldn't be happier about it.

Karen and her children are popular performers at weddings, at church, and for special events. She's taught her children that a consecrated person shares his or her talents willingly, that these talents are God-given, and that the purpose for developing them is to serve God and His children. Because of their mother's passion, being a musician has become a large part of the children's identities as well.

When our children see us consistently studying the scriptures, reading, writing, running, learning, performing music, creating art, or doing whatever we choose to do that is worthwhile and helps us grow, they will also value these things. We need to establish our homes as exciting and interesting places and make the things that matter most a priority—rather than allowing them to fall "at the mercy of things which matter least" (Ashley Montague as quoted in A. Theodore Tuttle, *Ensign*, Dec. 1971, 90).

Amid the distractions and commotion of our busy lives as mothers, true contentment comes from understanding the transcendent significance of motherhood and allowing that realization to affect our whole outlook on life, stewardship, and our mission as mothers. Developing a rich private life and sharing the talents we develop with our children can help us better appreciate and understand our calling and how to be content therewith. We become somebody because we *are* somebody—daughters of God. Author Marianne Williamson rightly expresses our potential as God's children:

> Our deepest fear is not that we are inadequate. Our deepest fear is that we are powerful beyond measure. It is our light, not our darkness that most frightens us. We ask ourselves, Who am I to be brilliant, gorgeous, talented, fabulous? Actually, who are you *not* to be? You are a child of God. Your playing small does not serve the world. There is nothing enlightened about shrinking so that other people won't feel insecure around you. We are all meant to shine, as children do. We were born to make manifest the glory of God that is within us. It's not just in some of us; it's in everyone. And as we let our own light shine, we unconsciously give other people permission to do the same. (*A Return to Love: Reflections on the Principles of a Course in Miracles*, 190–191)

ALLOWING OUR NATURES TO BE CHANGED THROUGH THE GRACE OF CHRIST

> "'That man is most truly great who is most Christlike. What you sincerely in your heart think of Christ will determine what you are, will largely determine what your acts will be. . . . By choosing him as our ideal, we create within ourselves a desire to be like Him, and to have fellowship with him.' If we think about Him long enough, we will begin to act like him, and if we act like Him long enough, we will truly become like Him."
> —David O. McKay as quoted in Gene R. Cook, "Charity: Perfect and Everlasting Love," *Ensign,* May 2002, 82, fn 33

Perhaps the most significant way of becoming fully content as mothers is to truly comprehend the nature of our Savior's Atonement and its efficacy in our lives. When we recognize and acknowledge our dependence on the Lord for our salvation, when we come to understand the divine nature of our role as mothers—who we are, and who our children are—our very natures will be changed through the grace of Christ. It is through this "mighty change of heart" that we can ultimately find lasting contentment.

Understanding the Savior's Atonement
Stephen Robinson, the author of *Believing Christ,* tells of an experience he and his wife, Janet, had that helped them better understand the Atonement of Jesus Christ. One year, while living in Pennsylvania, Janet went through an unbelievably busy and pressure-filled period. In addition to being the Relief

Society president, she was finishing her second college degree in accounting, was taking the CPA exam, had just started a job at a local accounting firm, and had recently given birth to their fourth baby.

One day, Brother Robinson writes, Janet just shut down as far as spiritual things went. She became very passive in her attitude towards the Church. When her counselors in Relief Society called her, she told them that they could do what they wanted—she had asked to be released from her calling. The worst part of it, Brother Robinson remembers, was that she wouldn't talk with him and tell him what was wrong. At last, after two weeks of his probing, Janet finally broke down and disclosed the following to her husband:

> All right. Do you want to know what's wrong? I'll tell you what's wrong—I can't do it anymore. I can't lift it. My load is just too heavy. I can't do all the things I'm supposed to. I can't get up at 5:30, and bake bread and sew clothes, and help the kids with their homework, and do my own homework, and make their lunches, and do the housework, and do my Relief Society stuff, and have scripture study, and do my genealogy, and write my congressman, and go to PTA meetings, and get our year's supply organized, and go to my stake meetings, and write the missionaries. . . .
>
> I try not to yell at the kids . . . but I can't seem to help it; I get mad, and I yell. So then I try not to get mad, but eventually I do. I try not to have hard feelings toward this person and that person, but I do. I'm just not very Christlike. No matter how hard I try to love everyone, I fail. I don't have the talent Sister X has, and I'm just not as sweet as Sister Y. Steve, I'm just not perfect—I'm never going to be perfect, and I just can't pretend anymore that I am. I've finally

admitted to myself that I can't make it to the celestial kingdom, so why should I break my back trying?

Brother Robinson says, "She just started naming, one after the other, all the things she couldn't do or couldn't do perfectly—all the individual bricks that had been laid on her back in the name of perfection until they had crushed the light out of her." He was truly baffled by this outburst. He writes that he married Janet because she was one of the finest, sweetest, most genuinely loving and selfless people he had ever known, and he knew her to be better than most. Ultimately, it occurred to him what the problem was:

> What I realized finally was that Janet did not completely understand the core of the gospel— the atonement of Christ. She knew the demands, but not the good news.
>
> Who would have thought that after all the meetings and lessons, after all the talks and testimonies and family home evenings, somehow the heart of the gospel had escaped her? She knew and believed everything except the most important part. You see, Janet was trying to save herself. She was trying to do it all with Jesus Christ as merely an advisor. Janet knew why Jesus can be called a coach, a cheerleader, an advisor, a teacher, the elder brother, the head of the Church, and even God. She understood all of that, but she didn't understand why he is called the *Savior.* . . .
>
> Part of the good news of the gospel is the knowledge that finally perfection comes, to those who desire it, through the atonement of Christ instead of solely through their own efforts. When we become one with Christ in the

gospel covenant, we gain access to *His* perfection. (14–17, 23)

As Latter-day Saint mothers, a lot *is* required of us. We are not a perfect people. As Janet Robinson learned, we cannot possibly save ourselves. When we finally recognize our truly desperate situation here in mortality and our need to be saved from it through the divine intervention and grace of Christ, we truly appreciate the sacrifice of the Atonement and the saving power extended to us. After all, "It is by grace that we are saved, after all we can do" (2 Nephi 25:23). In order for us to truly find contentment in our calling, we must reach out toward and accept this grace that is offered to us.

It is also critical that we understand that not only can we not *save* ourselves, but we cannot *change* ourselves either. To overcome deep, inherent tendencies and weaknesses that we have struggled with most of our lives will require more than just willpower. It will necessitate tapping deeply into the power of Christ's Atonement to conquer the "natural man." C.S. Lewis expresses it best:

> When I come to my evening prayers and try to reckon up the sins of the day, nine times out of ten the most obvious one is some sin against charity; I have sulked or snapped or sneered or snubbed or stormed. And the excuse that immediately springs to mind is that the provocation was so sudden or unexpected; I was caught off my guard, I had not time to collect myself. . . . Surely what a man does when he is taken off his guard is the best evidence for what sort of man he is? Surely what pops out before the man has time to put on a disguise is the truth? If there are rats in the cellar you are most likely to see them if you go in very suddenly. But the suddenness does not create rats: it only prevents

them from hiding. In the same way the sudden-
ness of provocation does not make me an ill-
tempered man: it only shows me what an
ill-tempered man I am. . . . Now that cellar is
out of reach of my conscious will. . . . I cannot,
by direct moral effort, give myself new motives.
After the first few steps . . . we realize that everything which really needs to be done in our souls
can be done only by God. (*Mere Christianity*,
164–165)

I have learned that to become fully content as a mother, I
need to develop a divine perspective of the significance of my
role and to allow my very nature to be changed through the
grace of Christ. Elder David A. Bednar makes it clear that this
process is a mighty—not minor—one. It is "a spiritual rebirth
and fundamental change of what we feel and desire, what we
think and do, and what we are. Indeed, the essence of the
gospel of Jesus Christ entails a fundamental and permanent
change in our very nature. . . . As we choose to follow the
Master, we choose to be changed" ("Ye Must Be Born Again,"
Ensign, May 2007, 20).

This "mighty change of heart" will not occur quickly or all
at once, since spiritual rebirth is a process and not an event. As
Elder Bednar further states, "Line upon line and precept upon
precept, gradually and almost imperceptibly, our motives, our
thoughts, our words, and our deeds become aligned with the
will of God" (ibid., 21). The Apostle Paul identifies the power
of the Spirit in this divine transformation: "But we all, with
open face beholding as in a glass the glory of the Lord, are
changed into the same image from glory to glory, even as by the
Spirit of the Lord" (2 Corinthians 3:18).

It is my understanding that when I align my will with
God's, my mission as a mother and God's mission as our Father
become very much the same: "For behold, this is my work and
my glory—to bring to pass the immortality and eternal life of

man" (Moses 1:39). Like our Heavenly Father, whose greatest desire is for the eternal progression of His children, my supreme aim as a mother is to raise honorable children who will bring glory to Him through the righteous actions they perform, the covenants they enter into, and the ordinances they complete while upon the earth. These children will continue to progress throughout eternity.

I have gained a testimony that as I seek to maintain this eternal perspective and weighty purpose amidst the day-to-day demands of family life, I can feel satisfied that my efforts *do* make a difference, that how I am raising my children really does matter, and that my commonplace, ordinary life may be elevated to that of the divine.

Keeping Our Eyes on the Shepherd
Phillip Keller's inspiring and insightful guide to Psalm 23, entitled *A Shepherd Looks at Psalm 23,* talks of how Keller grew up in East Africa and was later involved in every level of sheep management, including eight years as a sheep owner and rancher; in this book, he offers an intimate portrait of a shepherd's life and of the characteristics of sheep.

Keller makes the point that, for the most part, those who wrote the Bible were men of humble origin who penned under divine inspiration. These men were familiar with outdoor subjects and natural phenomena, in contrast with the general population of our day, who live in manmade environments and are unacquainted with matters such as livestock, crops, land, fruit, and wildlife. Since most of us are from urban settings and are generally unfamiliar with nature and outdoor topics—a phenomenon that has occurred only within the past one hundred and fifty years—we miss much of the truth taught in scripture. Keller offers his interpretation of the beloved 23rd Psalm through the perspective of a shepherd to help us thoroughly comprehend what David had in mind when he wrote it.

He notes that the phrase "he maketh me to lie down in green pastures" is a beloved Christian expression but is an almost impossible feat. For a shepherd to get his sheep to lie down, or be at rest, at least four requirements must be met: The sheep must be free of fear, free of friction with others of their kind, free of pests, and free from hunger.

If a shepherd can provide his sheep release from these anxieties, he makes it possible for them to lie down, rest, relax, and be content, quiet, and flourishing; otherwise the sheep continue to be agitated by these disturbing influences. Always uppermost in a caring shepherd's mind is the goal of meeting these needs so that his flock may be quiet, contented, and at peace.

Keller finds it extremely telling that it is the presence of the shepherd—the master, owner, and protector—that puts the sheep at ease as nothing else can. He draws the parallel, "In the Christian's life there is no substitute for the keen awareness that my Shepherd is nearby. There is nothing like Christ's presence to dispel the fear, the panic, the terror of the unknown" (26). As in our lives, the presence and the care of the Shepherd make all the difference in the contentment of His flock.

The Savior says, "I am come that they might have life, and that they might have it more abundantly" (John 10:10). I believe that the abundant life the Lord is offering is one of fulfillment, happiness, and true contentment. For mothers, this kind of life is only possible by keeping our eyes on the Master, *our* true Shepherd; otherwise, like the sheep, we too may be troubled by unsettling anxieties.

In a general Relief Society meeting, President Gordon B. Hinckley related the following story:

 Some years ago in the Salt Lake Tabernacle, Elder Marion D. Hanks conducted a panel discussion. Included in that panel was an attractive and able young woman, divorced, the mother of seven children then ranging in ages from 7 to 16. She said that one evening she went across the street to deliver something to a neighbor. Listen to her words as I recall them:

"As I turned around to walk back home, I could see my house lighted up. I could hear echoes of my children as I had walked out of the door a few minutes earlier. They were saying: 'Mom, what are we going to have for dinner?' 'Can you take me to the library?' 'I have to get some poster paper tonight.' Tired and weary I looked at that house and saw the light on in each of the rooms. I thought of all of those children who were home waiting for me to come and meet their needs. My burdens felt heavier than I could bear.

"I remember looking through tears toward the sky, and I said, 'Dear Father, I just can't do it tonight. I'm too tired. I can't face it. I can't go home and take care of all those children alone. Could I just come to You and stay with You for just one night? I'll come back in the morning.'

"I didn't really hear the words of reply, but I heard them in my mind. The answer was: 'No, little one, you can't come to me now. You would never wish to come back. But I can come to you.'"

After telling this true story, President Hinckley affirmed, "There are so very many like this young mother, who found herself in loneliness and desperation but was fortunate enough to have faith in the Lord, who could love her and help her" ("In the Arms of His Love," *Ensign*, Nov. 2006, 117).

Sometimes the Lord is the only one to whom we can turn when faced with such feelings of discouragement as mothers. He alone can cause us to feel "encircled about eternally in the arms of his love" (2 Nephi 1:15). Then, like a true Shepherd, He will lead us into green pastures and beckon us to lie down in quiet contentment.

Testifying of Motherhood
When my sister Jenny was attending college, she took an English class that concentrated on literary theory. The students learned to analyze literature from different critical approaches: formalism, historical criticism, structuralism, deconstructionism, and so forth.

One particular week, the class was reading short stories and analyzing them from a feminist point of view. This was also the week that our sister Cynthia gave birth to her sixth child. Jenny was invited, along with our parents, to be present at the birth. Initially, she was disgusted by the thought of the whole birth process—after all, she was only twenty years old and didn't know what to expect. Despite her hesitancy, she decided to attend anyway, and what she experienced was the most life-changing and spiritual experience she had ever had.

Jenny records:

> I remember being in the hospital room with my parents, Cynthia's husband, and her five other children. We were standing off to the side, and Cynthia was on the bed, covered by a sheet, so that the entire delivery was very appropriate and private. She had been given an epidural, so she was feeling fine. There were no screams of pain or anything of that nature. It was very peaceful and quiet.
>
> When it was time for her to deliver the baby, everything went perfectly. I don't remember the exact details, because I was so overcome by the feeling in the room. Tears flooded my eyes, and I believed that if I were to squint, I'd literally see angels. I truly felt the presence of spirits around me, and I suddenly understood the significance of what was happening at that moment. It was inspiring to catch a glimpse of the joy that Cynthia was experiencing and to feel the anticipation and

excitement in the room as we welcomed a beautiful, new baby into the world. I felt humbled to be there. I sensed that I was part of a miracle, standing as a witness of God's eternal plan of happiness.

I didn't talk much about it that night, but the spirit of the birth stayed with me into the next day as I went back to school. I attended my literary theory class, where we were analyzing Henrik Ibsen's play *The Doll's House* from a feminist perspective. Everyone, including the teacher, was discussing how women are and always have been suppressed—that their brains and talents are stifled by their role as mothers. It was a pretty intense conversation, and the whole class was basically mocking motherhood. The things they were saying were in complete contrast to my experience the night before.

After about thirty minutes of listening to these sentiments, I raised my hand. Because of the powerful events of the previous night, I felt strongly impressed to share my opinion. I solemnly expressed something to this effect: "I don't believe what you are all saying. Last night, I was able to attend the birth of my sister's sixth child, and the spirit I felt in that room is so different from the spirit I feel here now. All I know is that if I am ever able to be a mother, I will be the happiest, most fulfilled person that I can be."

The Spirit bore witness to the truth of my words. The entire mood in the room changed, and everyone became quiet. Although it was fifteen minutes early, the teacher dismissed the class.

When we summon our courage and stand by our convictions in defending and testifying of motherhood, the Spirit will in turn testify of truth, as it did in that English class that day. I would like to add my testimony to Jenny's that it *is* an honor and a privilege to be a mother. I know that raising up a family to the Lord is an essential part of my divine mission and that I can obtain no greater peace, happiness, or satisfaction through any other achievement in life. There is no glory or honor that can equal being the mother of a child well taught and trained so that he or she can return to the presence of our Father in Heaven. This is a choice blessing.

I am of the same mind as Alma when he reveals the basis of his testimony: "Behold, I testify unto you that I do know that these things whereof I have spoken are true. And how do ye suppose that I know of their surety? . . . Behold, I have fasted and prayed many days that I might know these things of myself. And now I do know of myself that they are true; for the Lord God hath made them manifest unto me by his Holy Spirit" (Alma 5:45, 46).

Honoring the Divine Natures of Our Children

Sometimes, when I am overwhelmed or discontent in my role as mother, I imagine being in the premortal realm, surrounded by my children—mighty and faithful spirits, who have covenanted with their Heavenly Father to remain true to the divinity within them. I immediately experience a deep respect for each of them, and I feel humbled by the weighty responsibility of raising them in righteousness.

Several years ago, when our oldest son, Covey, was around eleven years old, he did something that made me very angry. I don't even remember what he did that upset me so much, but I distinctly recall overreacting and sending him to his room. After about an hour, I went downstairs to his room with the intent of further reprimanding him. Yet, when I opened his door and saw him lying on his bed, I was *literally* given a glimpse of his noble character. For just a moment, my soul comprehended who he truly was, and I felt overpowered by a profound love and reverence for him. The Spirit chastised me, inquiring, "Do you have any idea who this boy is?"

Not as dramatically, but without doubt, I have experienced similar impressions about each one of my children through the years. As we read in Romans, "The Spirit itself beareth witness with our spirit, that we are the children of God" (Romans 8:16). I am so grateful to have been taught on these occasions of the magnitude of my stewardship and to feel a true sense of the valiant nature of the children with whom my husband and I have been entrusted—each a literal spirit son or daughter of God.

Herein is where contentment in motherhood is ultimately found: understanding who our children are and honoring their divine natures and parentage. When we fully comprehend that we are stewards over these "children of the promise" (Romans 9:8) and that we must give an accounting of them to God, the Father of us all, we develop a deeper awareness of the significance of our responsibility, and we desire to be faithful and wise in this stewardship. Our children are promised *peace,* and we are assured *joy* as we teach them diligently and bring them up in light and truth: "And all thy children shall be taught of the Lord; and great shall be the peace of thy children" (3 Nephi 22:13). Truly, "I have no greater joy than to hear that my children walk in truth" (3 John 1:4).

This, then, is contentment—"the peace of God, which passeth all understanding" (Philippians 4:7). Let us hold fast to it as we mother our children.

SELECTED BIBLIOGRAPHY

Ashton, Norma B. "For Such a Time as This," in *The Best of Women's Conference: Selected Talks from 25 Years of BYU Women's Conferences.* Salt Lake City: Bookcraft, 2000.

Bahr, Kathleen and Cheri A. Loveless. "The Meaning and Blessings of Family Work," in *Strengthening Our Families: An In-Depth Look at the Proclamation on the Family,* ed. David C. Dollahite. Salt Lake City: Deseret Book Co., 2000.

Bennett, Jeanette. "Would-Be First Lady Is a First-Rate Lady," *Utah Valley Magazine,* July–August 2008.

Bennett, William J. *Our Sacred Honor.* New York: Simon & Schuster, 1997.

Benson, Ezra Taft. *The Teachings of Ezra Taft Benson.* Salt Lake City: Deseret Book Co., 1988.

Benson, Lee. "Treadmill Lets Mother of 3 Stay in Race," *Deseret News,* 16 July 2008.

Cather, Willa. *My Antonia.* New York: Random House, 1994.

Covey, Sean. *Fourth Down and Life to Go.* Salt Lake City: Bookcraft, 1991.

Covey, Stephen R. *The 8th Habit: From Effectiveness to Greatness.* New York: Free Press, 2004.

_____. *The Seven Habits of Highly Effective People: Restoring the Character Ethic.* New York: Simon and Schuster, 1989.

Eleni, directed by Peter Yates, New Line Home Video, Nov. 1985, videocassette/DVD.

Garland, Judy. Found online at http://thinkexist.com/quotation/always_be_a_first-rate_version_of_yourself/210051.html

Holland, Patricia. *A Quiet Heart.* Salt Lake City: Bookcraft, 2000.

Johnson, Sherrie. *Spiritually Centered Motherhood.* Salt Lake City: Bookcraft, 1983.

Keller, Phillip. *A Shepherd Looks at Psalm 23.* Michigan: Zondervan, 1970.

Kenison, Katrina. *Mitten Strings for God.* New York: Time Warner, 2002.

Kimball, Spencer W. *Teachings of Presidents of the Church: Spencer W. Kimball,* Salt Lake City: The Church of Jesus Christ of Latter-day Saints, 2006.

_____. *The Teachings of Spencer W. Kimball,* ed. Edward L. Kimball. Salt Lake City: Bookcraft, 1982. Cited as *Teachings.*

Klein, Gerda Weissmann. *All But My Life.* New York: Hill and Wang, 1995.

Lewis, C. S. *Mere Christianity.* New York: Macmillan, 1960.

Lindbergh, Anne Morrow. *Gift from the Sea.* New York: Pantheon Books, 2003.

Maxwell, Neal A. *We Will Prove Them Herewith,* Salt Lake City: Deseret Book Co., 1982.

_____. In "This Week in Church History: 25 Years Ago," *Church News,* Feb. 16, 2008.

McConkie, Bruce R. *Mormon Doctrine,* 2nd ed. Salt Lake City: Deseret Book Co., 1966.

Mother Teresa. Found online at http://www.scu.edu/ethics/architects-of-peace/Teresa/lesson.html

Peck, Scott M. *The Road Less Traveled: A New Psychology of Love, Traditional Values and Spiritual Growth.* New York: Simon and Schuster, 1978.

Robinson, Stephen E. *Believing Christ: The Parable of the Bicycle and Other Good News.* Salt Lake City: Deseret Book, 1992.

Shaw, George Bernard. "George Bernard Shaw Quotes," found online at http://thinkexist.com/quotation/life_isn-t_about_ finding_yourself-life_is_about/8906.html

Smith, Joseph F. *Gospel Doctrine: Selections from the Sermons and Writings of Joseph F. Smith.* Salt Lake City: Deseret Book Co., 1977.

Suzuki, Sinichi. Found online at http://thinkexist.com/quotation/the_real_essence_of_art_turned_out_to_be_not/145105.html.

Ueland, Brenda. *If You Want to Write: A Book about Art, Independence, and Spirit.* Saint Paul: Graywolf Press, 1987.

Wilder, Thornton. *Our Town.* New York: Harper and Row, 1957.

Williamson, Marianne. *A Return to Love: Reflections on the Principles of a Course in Miracles.* New York: Harper Collins, 1992.

Winters, Charlene Renberg. "The Art of Family," *BYU Magazine,* Spring 2007.

ABOUT THE AUTHOR

Maria Covey Cole is a homemaker and the mother of five children. She served a mission in Dublin, Ireland, and completed a political internship in Washington, D.C. She holds a bachelor's degree in English from Brigham Young University and a master's degree in educational studies from the University of Utah. She is a frequent speaker at BYU Education Week. Maria finds contentment in reading, writing, running, and raising children.